INDIE WRITER UNBOXED

The Three-Year, No-bestseller Plan For Making A Living From Your Fiction Book 4

PATTY JANSEN

Get FREE ebooks

Visit pattyjansen.com
to sign up for Patty's mailing list. You get four series starter ebooks for free!

ONE

This is a book from my heart

THE RUSH OF EXCITEMENT IS OVER.

You've published a book, and you're working on the next. Maybe you've published a number of books. They might be selling fine (what "fine" means will depend on the individual), or you might be unhappy with sales.

You are now a self-published author. Your books are out there for all to see.

But inevitably questions of doubt rear their ugly heads: is this all there is? Do I really have to spend so much time marketing? Is it meant to be so hard? What's next? How do I advance my career? How do I even make a career out of this when my books don't sell as much as I'd like to? How do I get out of this rut?

Don't worry, this book is for you!

In this book, we will join four writers who are just like you, and follow them through their trials and tribulations as they learn to cope with life as self-published author.

So what sort of book is this?

In 2017, I published *Self-publishing Unboxed*, *Mailing Lists Unboxed* and *Going Wide Unboxed*. I always had thoughts about a fourth book, one that took a holistic look at what goes on in a writer's career post-publishing. It would be a book that attempted to make sense of the cycle of elations and frustrations, the ups and downs you can only understand once you've published.

Many self-publishers and their communities focus on targeted, practical subjects that you can act on immediately. A lot of these projects are incredibly short-term, concerned only with immediate profits or gains. To be honest, this is the entire nature of the industry. Fed up with waiting for someone else to take months (or years) to decide about their books, writers take matters into their own hands. Of course they're a little impatient.

When you're wondering what to do for a book launch, you don't exactly feel like thinking about the things you do now that can influence your career next year. You want an easy path to as many sales as possible and you want it now.

Not that I'm immune to the short-term trend.

We're consumed by publishing schedules, deadlines, return on investment and mailing lists. It's about efficiency. We like that. Solving problems is our thing. Hands on is the way we like to do our business.

But sometimes, it's worth taking a step back and thinking: where is this all going? Am I on the main line or the sidetrack? Am I making the type of progress I want to make, and what is this life doing to me, to my finances and my happiness?

So this book is about you, the writer and all the different ways you can tackle your progress—or lack thereof. It's a book that discusses the options from the point of view of the person who has to do all of it: you.

Because the most important ingredient in your writing career is your ability to keep writing books.

The path you take in your career is a reflection of your personality, your writing speed, the way you like promoting, the way you interact with readers and many other factors related to writing or to your life in general.

Do you want to be full-time but it seems forever out of reach? Did you go full-time, but are not happy? Do you suffer from crippling self-doubt? Do you feel burnt out with the ever-increasing pressure to produce books at a faster and faster pace? Or do you feel that everyone else seems to have more luck and better sales than you? Do you worry that making money seems to become harder every day? Do you feel you can't keep up? Did you have success early on but your sales are slipping every day?

If you current situation makes you unhappy, it's time to reconsider your processes and habits. You need to look at yourself and decide what sort of career you want. You need to cut out a new space for yourself. Most importantly, you will need to discard some of your activities that cause stress or that don't deliver results.

You may need to re-examine your definition of success.

Not looking after your emotional stability or trying too desperately to keep up with the Joneses can send you down nasty rabbit holes, where you will meet with the many different ways in which you can sabotage your career. Self-doubt, self-rejection, envy are all emotional states that can seriously affect your ability to write, as well as damaging your general happiness.

Sitting down for hours at the computer can be quite detrimental to your health.

When all those things—your workspace, your financial security, your home space, your mental space—are not aligned, your productivity drops and your morale falls.

This book is about how to navigate the right space, and how to determine whether something is or isn't going to work for you. It is about how to avoid difficult situations and how to keep yourself happy and writing.

It's a book I've written because I've lived many of the situations or have seen them happen, time and time again, in front of my eyes.

When I first started writing chapters for this book, straight after I finished *Going Wide Unboxed*, I ended up talking to the readers too much. I didn't like it, because this is not a book where anyone has definitive answers. It's not a book of how-tos and lectures.

It was not until I stumbled upon the current format—to show writing careers through the eyes of four imaginary writers—that the content "felt" right.

So let's dive in.

TWO

In Which I Rain on Your Parade

I DON'T LIKE BEING a Negative Nelly. That said, some things about writing careers need to be talked about. The self-published writing community is one of great positivity. It's full of can-do people with plans and hopes. The sky is the limit; the world is your oyster. That sort of thing.

No more gatekeepers. We can be our own boss. We don't need to conform to publishers' narrow definitions of genre or wait for their **OK**.

It's liberating.

It's exciting.

But it can also be scary and depressing.

It's not going to be an easy ride for everyone.

It's probably not even going to be an easy ride for most people.

Yet those negative things can be kind of taboo in the community. No sales? Easy. Change your cover; change your blurb! Run some ads; write another book. Those are all things you can do. But the truth is that it's unlikely to have the desired effect. And what then? You spent a lot of money ordering new covers for your books and pinning your hopes on a rebranding, but they still don't sell in great numbers.

So in the next few chapters, I'll go on being a Negative Nelly for just a bit. It's all in the name of tough love and managing expectations. And a little tough love never hurt anyone.

I will spend the next four chapters raining on your parade, so that I can get the raining over with and can talk about what to do about these issues later.

It's now time to meet our four imaginary writers to illustrate a couple of bad places you can find yourself in after having written a few books. Likely, you'll find a bit of all four writers in your own situation.

A note: these people don't exist. I've cobbled them together from writers I've met in the real world. They're not real people, but they might as well be.

THREE

Tom: Unicorns Farting Rainbows

TOM (62) HAS BEEN READING his chosen genre for a long time, and has been writing for quite a long time, too. He submitted to a few agents and magazines years ago, even got some encouraging rejections, but has never sold anything.

Tom feels disillusioned with the state of current publishing, being unable to find any books he likes on the shelves of recently published books. So he has decided to write those books himself.

Tom writes Science Fiction.

Tom is semi-retired. He is a trained chemical engineer, has worked for a long time, and is confident in his abilities.

After his wife Helena was diagnosed with a debilitating illness that's slowly killing her, he took a redundancy package to enable him to look after her. But since that's not a full-time occupation, he's been motivated to do something about his long-held dream to write.

He chose to self-publish this time, because he read about other people making good money doing it.

Tom has published four books. Because Tom is a thorough fellow, he read up on publishing before he pushed the button, and he had his books edited and supplied them with nice covers. His books are even in a series: three in one series and one book in the next series.

Except the books don't sell very well. Early on, he sold a few hundred copies of the first book, less than half of that of the second book, and less again of the third. For a beginner, this is actually quite admirable. He must be doing something right. But Tom is not really happy.

So he did the right thing and started another series. To his dismay, the first book of that series sells even worse.

What gives?

He's done all the right things, and look at his books! They're so much better than the stuff that inhabits the top 100. The fellow who ran a workshop that Tom attended before publishing told the students that all you needed to do was make sure you put out a quality product. He did that, and now the books are ranking in the telephone numbers.

He doesn't get it. They're all just selling unicorns farting rainbows.

Tom hates marketing because none of his ads ever seem to work when he tries. He detests book spam.

He doesn't like spending money. He has a website which he built himself, doesn't like newsletters, although he's got one which he uses infrequently, because people don't really seem to connect with him there.

He feels dejected and reluctant to continue his second series, and even more reluctant to start something new. He knows the books are good because he's got good reviews, and cream should rise to the top, right?

FOUR

Emily: Let Me off the Hamster Wheel

EMILY (32) IS A WRITER of cosy mysteries and paranormal romance.

She's newly divorced, without children. When she found herself without work, she started writing.

Her first cosy mystery book sold really well by a kind of fluke, because she'd never written anything before, so she wrote a second book in the series, that also sold really well, so she wrote a third book and then her series really took off. After six books, she was heartily sick of the series. There was nothing more to tell.

So she started another series, which seemed to do fine for a while.

Emily noticed that each time she released a new book, her sales would jump, so the answer was obviously to write more. She followed some productivity courses to the point where she could comfortably write a new book every couple of weeks.

Emily doesn't market much, because she doesn't have the time for that. Besides, bringing out a new book is the best marketing, right?

But it's starting to catch up with her. She's running out of ideas, she feels like she's repeating herself and, if that wasn't bad enough, her sales per book keep dropping. With fifty books, she is now earning the same as she did with twenty-five.

Should she change tack?

She can write quickly, so she tried a different genre, paranormal romance, under a pen name. Emily can write, so the sales were encouraging at first, but then tailed off. Then she discovered that having two pen names means doing two lots of keeping up with everything. The obvious route seemed to let someone else take over one of the pen name as ghostwriter or collaborator. That worked for a while, but Emily still needs to generate the ideas. And she feels she is fast heading for that wall where either she's going to run out of ideas or the amount of work she has to do is going to put her in hospital.

She can't write any faster. In fact, she would love to write a bit slower. She would like to write in a different genre, but her fans keep asking her for books in the same series, including the series she now hates so much she can't stand the look of it. In fact, every time she opens those books, she cringes with the clunky prose and overall terrible writing.

Emily lost the enjoyment of writing, and she wants to find it. She wants her life back, where she could do other things at night, take time off and, heavens, even go on a date.

She wants off the hamster wheel.

FIVE

Jack: Feeding the Beast

JACK (35) WAS TRAINED as a graphic designer and worked for a web design company for a while before quitting his job when his third book sold really well.

He writes a couple of books a year. He writes crime fiction and mysteries.

Early in his career, he sold two books to a medium-sized press, but his other books are all self-published.

Jack has a successful crime series, which is not finished, and is working on a police procedural series, also not finished. He also has some standalone books, a psychological thriller and two spy thrillers, and his earlier work with the publisher is detective fiction. He has since managed to get his rights back for these books.

So he has a decent stable of books, even if they're disjointed.

Through some fluke, his third book—the police procedural—sold really well, but it didn't spill over to his other books as much as he hoped. And the time when you can just publish a book and have it sell well is over.

Jack understands that in order to make money, you have to spend money. He got involved in pay-per-click ads early, and he considers himself quite good at them.

The problem is, the cost keeps increasing. He's spending 50 cents out of every dollar earned in advertising, which, when combined with the production cost per book, doesn't leave him much room. His sales might be decent, but he's spending more and more on ads, leaving him with less and less income.

He's also spending more time looking after his ads. At one stage, he paid someone else to do it, but that also grew too expensive, so he's gone back to doing it himself, which gives him less time to write. Meanwhile, readers keep asking him for the next book in those series he plans to write and some he doesn't.

Jack is fearful that his costs will keep going up and his income won't keep pace. He's worried about the time he spends marketing, but he's afraid that if he does less, his sales will collapse.

Jack lives with his partner Tony, who has a low-paying job. Between the two, they can pay for the rent of their reasonably upmarket apartment, maintain their old car, and pay all the bills. But there is no money for extras, including the dog they dearly want.

SIX

Lucy: Ready To Quit

LUCY (45) HAS WRITTEN a number of books, some of which have sold quite well. She writes romance and has written both historical and contemporary romance.

She's not a huge seller, but makes a decent middle-income wage.

She is a very social person, who runs a reader group on Facebook with an active community focus.

Lucy also has a lot of interests and she runs a Facebook group for animal rights activists. In this capacity, she has clashed with a few people, and now she is convinced that those people are trying, in her words, to "tear her down" by leaving one-star reviews on her books. She has complained to Amazon numerous times, and has been ignored. After this happened, she asked her readers to support her. Then another writer in one of her groups told her she was seeing fairies, and now her friend group is split, and people are arguing with each other.

On top of that, her husband is making snide remarks about the time she spends writing, even though he likes the money she brings in.

All this is affecting her ability to write. She feels like she is continuously putting out fires and she is simply not enjoying it anymore. This seeps through in her writing, and the last book wasn't as well received as the one before that. She's still making money, but the time she spends stalking reviewers on Amazon pages and Facebook groups makes her sick.

Sooner or later, she'll come to a public page where someone will have called her a hack and a fraud. She never took any formal writing training, so she is a fraud, but she wonders why people need to be so mean and punish her through her books. Don't they understand that she works hard, and didn't their mothers tell them: If you can't say anything nice, then say nothing at all?

Lucy lives with her husband Sam and has two school-aged girls. She hasn't worked for about ten years, and started writing because she needed something to do with herself.

SEVEN

What Is Success Anyway?

EARLY ON IN HIS CAREER, Tom did an online course by a well-known self-published writer whose name is Luke.

Attached to the course was a Facebook group in which a couple of other writers were vocal. They all seemed very knowledgeable and businesslike, and all sold very well. They talked about hiring assistants and going to events overseas.

Tom saw this as an encouragement for what he could achieve with his hard work. He saw "do this and this and then you will earn this much". He was not afraid of a bit of work, and he did the work.

He hired an editor and cover designer who both came with recommendations and made sure his books looked good.

But they still didn't sell half as well as the books of those writers.

He put the question why to the group.

Some people talked about the covers. They looked nice, they said, but how well did they reflect the genre?

Other people talked about the blurbs. They were a bit dry, they said. There wasn't a character to sympathise with.

The books are old-style science fiction, Tom replied, it's about the ideas.

One person said it was all down to luck. The moment you put out a book, you have very little control over how well—or how poorly—it will sell.

And a whole bunch of people jumped onto that commenter to say how wrong that was. That if only Tom had a big mailing list and this dreadful thing called an *audience* or, even more dreadful, a *platform*, he'd have no trouble selling his books. He just needed to find his readers.

But Tom doesn't have a big audience. In fact, he doesn't really like the mailing lists and abhors social media.

He's not into list-swapping or giving free books away, because he wants his fans to be genuine, except he can see that if no one reads his books, there won't be any fans.

Then one writer pointed out that Tom's books had sold a few hundred copies, and that this was much better than hers had sold, and she pointed Tom to a reasonably recent survey by Freebooksy, which showed that the vast majority of authors who earn six figures a year have more than thirty books.

This put things in perspective for him.

Those writers who were so vocal in the group, being helpful about sharing their sales and methods? They were flukes.

Most group members were the silent majority, neither as successful nor as keen to talk about their (lack of) success. Tom is, in fact, perfectly normal.

He feels a bit stupid, because he should have known that. Every so often, articles come out saying how little the average author makes. Self-publishing shortens the odds somewhat, but that is because of the lack of layers and layers of middlemen taking their slice out of a book's cover price.

Even when Luke started the course, he said that it was a hard industry and that if you wanted to be certain about making money and making it quickly, you should take a paid job.

After all the other things he talked about, like his success and the success of his friends, the reality check was so easy to forget. The talk was so tempting. Write a book, give it the professional treatment and watch the cash roll in.

You must spend money to make money.

If only it really were that simple.

But first maybe Tom needs to examine his definition of success. What does he need and want, and what is his dream?

Some people consider success as simply having published a book.

Many people never finish the book they started, so it's a kind of success, but Tom thinks that's lame. There must be a more ambitious definition.

Having a bestseller is success. That's Tom's dream: being able to say that a book was a #1 bestseller or made it to the USA Today bestseller list, even if a lot of people say readers don't care that much about those things.

But Luke also said that getting a bestseller is a fluke, especially very early in your career. He said it was much better to produce a number of books that sell at a consistent level that respond well to advertising and slowly chip away at this whole success thing than to have a flash-in-the-pan and then be at a loss as to how to repeat it.

But Tom glossed over all those words that Luke said in the

course. He heard, "You can be a bestseller," and forgot about the "can" part. Looking back on it, it's almost amusing how he fell for this clever advertising to sell the course. It was useful, to be sure, but the course was still being sold to him with the promise of success. It taught him tricks of the trade. About success, it said little.

What Tom really wants is some extra money for him and Helena to visit Helena's brother before she becomes too ill to travel. He will settle for that as a short-term goal.

Other people may want to quit their job and some seek to supplement their income. Some may simply want a little extra on top of a pension. For some people, publishing is not about money at all.

However, Tom now understands that he has poor control over how well his books sell and how they rank, so he should quit feeling bad about the writers whose books do better than his. Of course it's easier said than done.

He would love to earn some money and he has a dreadful time constraint.

Tom would be much happier if he took measuring success in small, month-by-month steps. Has he earned back the cost of producing the books yet?

When he has, he might look at the next step: can he afford to pay for covers for his new series in advance? Does he have the money to take a short course, attend a workshop or con, or ask advice from an advertising expert?

Tom should try to budget a percentage of his income on ads. He makes a few hundred dollars a month, but even if he only makes $40, he might spend $10 on a promotion. He can spend it on a smaller site or save it for something bigger.

But he can also try to reduce his spending. If I were him, I'd keep the editor, but rather than go with the really expensive cover designer, I'd look for someone who still does really nice work but is a bit cheaper.

If he and his wife were younger and healthy, he might also have liked to move to a cheaper place. Why do you think that quite a few writers live in rural areas or low-cost countries? Why do you think people sell their houses and decide to live cheaply for a year?

You can control your expenses much more than you can control your sales.

You can budget yourself into being a full-time author.

Unfortunately, that's not a viable option for Tom and, besides, he has some savings and only needs to bridge three years until he can access his retirement income. He's not terribly worried about surviving.

But he feels like he's treading water, and time is ticking.

EIGHT

Keep Learning

JACK IS A PERFECT EXAMPLE of how much a career is a moving target.

He started off as a graphic-design professional, got a deal from a publisher, self-published, and sold really well for a while before moving into heavy advertising.

Jack knows that he has to keep learning or he will grow stale, and before he knows it he will have been left behind by everyone else.

Learning involves a good amount of keeping track of methods to write better stories. Learning also involves the latest trends in your genre and the most effective marketing methods.

He's a member of the same Facebook group as Tom, and he sees a comment by Tom that disturbs him.

Tom says about learning marketing: Marketing is all rubbish. It doesn't work for my books anyway.

Jack challenges him to state what he's tried and what he's been learning.

A good book markets itself, Tom says.

Yes, if only that were true. Jack pulls up an example of a book everyone can see has issues that is better-ranked than Tom's. That's marketing right there, he says, and goes on: I'd hate to know how much these people spend on ads. You can absolutely advertise your book to rank well. You only need to learn how.

An intense discussion ensues.

Jack says:

The more you get into commercial publishing the more you will understand that even writing craft and marketing are intertwined.

The type of story you tell, the type of sentences you use, the type of point-of-view character you choose, will influence major choices such as what genre you put your book in, and that determines how well you can market it.

But, Tom says, those genres are just rubbish perpetuated by publishers. I'm free of that. You can't classify my books.

And Jack says:

Nope, Tom, mate, you write science fiction, and I don't think you understand the concept of genre as shorthand for a type of book readers want to read.

Readers don't want to have to read the blurb to see what they're getting. Neither do readers want to think they're getting a space opera, only to find that the story is a family drama with a very strong literary bent.

Your craft and familiarity with other books in your genre is of vital importance. Craft is storytelling, and it ties in with genre, including established tropes you can break, and ones you can't without upsetting readers in your genre.

You have to learn to let your readers know that your story is kind-of the same as one they've read before, but different. It's not as easy as it sounds.

At this point someone makes a very cutting remark about Jack's scattershot catalogue that gets deleted by the group's moderators, because it's a "personal attack" and Jack had not asked for advice.

But he gets angry anyway, because the maker of the remark really doesn't know anything about his situation, about how much time he spends researching his books and improving his writing. He's taking his career seriously, and he sells better than the upstart writer, so what does he know?

But the remark burrows under his skin. He *knows* that he should write book 2 and 3 in the series of the book that still sells well. But, he says, you have to consider your ability to keep producing books at a rate that is comfortable for you, and find a way to measure success that is not going to leave you feeling depressed.

At this point, he leaves the discussion, because he has work to do, and doesn't want to draw his own work further into the discussion.

All this talk about not feeling depressed is not easy, Emily says. The rest of the publishers are moving at a ridiculous speed. How can you keep up when groups of people are publishing a book a week?

A book a week? That's ridiculous, says Tom.

Others confirm that there are groups of people doing just that, and not just in romance either.

Lucy says: The answer is you can't keep up, but you can find your own audience.

She is very good at that. Her readers are loyal, even if they sometimes also make her feel stressed out.

Talk to the readers, she says. Send your fans a survey to ask them what they want. Give them a choice of two books to download, by other writers if necessary, and see what they choose. And then go and write in that subgenre.

This make Tom feel more depressed, because he doesn't want to talk to anyone. He just sends new releases to his list—if he remembers.

Emily doesn't even have a list, so she feels even more depressed. Yet something twigs with her. She really doesn't know much about the people who read her books. Not that she needs to know exactly who they are, but it would be useful to know where they hang out. For example, she hears that Facebook attracts mostly older folk today and that the young crowd are all on Instagram. Do her books appeal to older or younger people? She's always assumed she was writing for "people like me" but she could be completely wrong about that.

Before signing off for the day, she makes a note that she puts on the pin board on the wall above her desk. She hasn't used the board in ages. It still displays some pieces of paper with plans for books she published years ago and outlines for other books she never ended up writing.

On the bright yellow note, she writes **KEEP LEARNING**, with underneath the points: craft, advertising, mailing list, and her bugbear: research.

She never does enough research. There just isn't the time, and cosy mysteries are not known for their factual correctness. It's all about the story, right?

But it does bug her that sometimes reviewers find issues that she really should have checked. Peanuts grow under the ground, not on branches. Even in her paranormal romance—a genre where everything is made up—she managed to screw up the moon cycle. That was embarrassing. If you write about werewolves, you should know about the moon phases.

Someone else said something to her the other day. He said: if they see something that annoys them, most people will just close the book and never say anything. The ones who write reviews are only a small percentage.

What if her flubbing is catching up with her? It was easy when she started, because her first book caught the wind. But now there may be other, newer, less formulaic and overall better-researched books for readers to buy.

Tom is pretty certain that he's already done a lot of learning about his subject and his time submitting to traditional presses has prepared him well for writing. He just needs to learn how to market.

Jack only feels he needs to learn how not to put his foot in it. He's a real Jack: Jack of all trades, master of none. Except maybe advertising, but without a good product to sell, advertising is going to be extremely expensive. Maybe that's what's wrong with his books. They plain suck.

NINE

Everything Goes Wrong

AFTER THAT EMBARRASSING DISCUSSION, Jack is annoyed with himself. He really needs to write books, not faff around in Facebook groups.

But after seeing off Tony to his boring menial job, he sits around staring at his screen. He ignores his ads. He makes coffee, he does the washing, makes more coffee, decides they need milk and goes to the shops and before he knows it, only an hour remains before he expects Tony to come back.

He knows he needs to write more books, but it's just so easy to set up a few ads. But those ads deliver an ever-thinner margin and he's not sure how long they will continue to be successful. His rankings are slipping all the time. It's not a long-term strategy. He needs to write something new.

So he goes back to the group.

He writes: For writers who write more than four books a year: how do you do it?

This is right up Emily's alley. Even though she's sick of writing so many books, she has some advice.

Plan your books, she says.

Jack is not a planner.

I wasn't a planner either, she says, but if you want to increase your production, you need to plan, take it from me.

OK, he wants to know: how detailed?

She says that she writes a short paragraph for each chapter and then fills it in. She says she also knows people who make more detailed outlines.

Jack struggles with an outline for the next hour. He's never outlined, hated writing a synopsis for his traditionally published books, and he knows that when he's writing the story, it will go in directions that are irrelevant to the outline. Writing the outline feels like a giant waste of time. But he completes it anyway, and hates it, so he writes another, which he also hates.

When Tony comes home, tired from filling shelves, Jack is about ready to fling his computer out the window.

Tom has heard Jack's comments that learning about the competition is part of marketing. He has his next book mapped out, but he doesn't want to start writing it for fear that he's wasting his time.

So he spends the day looking at the Amazon top 100 in Science Fiction. He reads through the Look Inside samples of a lot of the books and hates most of them. They're neither well-written nor interesting. He does find some books to buy, but none of them are written by his self-published colleagues.

Then it's time to take Helena to a medical appointment. In the car, he talks about his frustration. He doesn't like the fiction that's being published.

She says, "You always said that the moment you stopped enjoying your job, you'd retire."

That's true. He had said that, and in the end the choice had been made for him.

He asks her why she brings this up.

Helena says, "It seems to me that if you don't enjoy what you're trying to write, maybe you need to write something else. You can't change those books in the top 100. If you want to be there, you need to write in that style, or whatever those writers are doing, or if you really hate today's science fiction so much, write something else."

That shakes him, because that's not what he means at all. He doesn't hate science fiction; he just . . . doesn't like what's being published.

But even he and Jack are doing better than Lucy.

She is supposed to be writing a new book, but two months ago, she agreed to organise a giveaway and now she needs to set it all up and communicate with the writers who are taking part.

Have you ever tried organising a group of writers? It's like herding cats. And some of them are so rude. She's still having an argument with this woman whose book she rejected for the giveaway, because the cover was amateurish and ugly. Lucy told her she'd be accepted next time if she got a more professional cover, but the woman is complaining about not having money and Lucy discriminating against her.

So while arguing with this woman, Lucy emails the other writers, collects the money for the prize, sets up the web page, and then needs to get her children from school. They've run out of bread so she needs to get that as well, even if the shops are on the way back home for her husband, and they won't need the bread until tomorrow morning. She asked him once before, and he was most miffed.

When she comes back, there is another whiny email from the

slighted woman—seriously why don't these people get a life?—and now someone has left a one-star review on her best-selling book.

It's only one line and says, "Couldn't get into it." That is surely another one of those troll reviews. It doesn't even come from a verified purchase, so it's just someone who read the sample online. Why do people do this?

Emily sits in her living room at the dining table. She can sit there because no one else uses it, and she doesn't need to cook because no one is eating at home, except her cat.

She is in the middle of her most recent book, and she hates it. From having written so many books, she knows it's common to hate every book when you're in that horrible middle. Usually it all gets resolved at the end.

But this time, she feels different. The story feels stale. It feels like she has written this book before. It feels like the readers also know this, and they're deserting her.

Emily checks her sales figures once a day, and when she finally does that, her sales are slightly better than yesterday. Still not a figure she is happy with, even though her last release was two weeks ago.

She picks up the cat and carries him to the window. From her third floor apartment, she can see into the street and into a cafe and fruit and veg shop across the road.

A couple walks hand in hand over the footpath. A bus stops, letting out a few people in business clothing.

Emily feels detached. She made her 5000 words for today, but it no longer feels fresh, or even like an achievement. She doesn't understand why people have so much trouble writing that much. It's easy. It's the rest that she has trouble with.

TEN

Never Mind the Joneses

LUCY HAS BEEN WORRYING about that review all during dinner. Her book has a 4.7 star average and she doesn't want that to go down any further. She's sure that the person who posted the latest review belongs to a group of trolls that's been bothering her in her animal activist group.

So after dinner, she sifts through a few thousand members of that group to see if she can find anyone she disagreed with recently.

At any rate, she files a complaint with Amazon, but knows—having complained before—that they never do anything. She doesn't understand why not. It's clear this person never even read the book. Going back through their reviews, Lucy can see that the reviewer has been posting lots of short reviews, most of them one or two stars.

She asks for advice from the writer group.

There is nothing you can do, they say.

One or two people even suggest that she should forget about it and stop looking at her reviews.

How can you just conclude this is a troll? Another writer asks. I can't see anything that points that way.

But she didn't even read the book, Lucy says.

The reply: people write these reviews all the time. People are entitled to say what they want about your book. You can't stop them.

Lucy asks: So you think I should just let them abuse me? I won't stand for it.

It's not abuse. It's the reviewer's right to say this, a number of members tell her.

But it's unfair, Lucy says.

Yes, if they haven't read the book, it is, says one of the best-selling authors in the group. But I try not to let it affect me, because if I do, the reviewer wins, because I spend my time obsessing about their words and not writing. I won't allow them to have that power over me.

And that, finally, is something that strikes home. In the last few days, Lucy has done little except worry about reviews and trolls and keeping all the people in that giveaway she's running happy. She should be writing.

Jack is watching the discussion in the group. In another browser tab, he's checking his ranking, as he has done a few dozen times today.

Tony can see from Jack's face that the news isn't good.

Jack feels ashamed to tell his partner that his expensive ads are failing, but Tony isn't dumb.

He tells Jack: I don't really care what ranking your books are at.

Ranking is money, Jack says, without taking his eyes off the screen.

Tony holds a cup of coffee in between Jack's face and the computer.

No, he says. Money in the bank is money. Ranking is comparing yourself with other people. If you were second to the best crime writer in the world—what is the dude's name again?—you'd gladly be second. It wouldn't matter. What matters is what they put in your bank account.

Jack insists: But that's related to rank.

It stresses you out, Tony says. I don't like that; it makes you grumpy. Like it's so important that some so-and-so all the way in Canada ranked better than you. Who cares?

But Jack cares. He knows that people out there are watching him. People from his days of traditional publishing, who said that self-publishing would finish his career. People who would gloat over every point his rank slips as a way to prove that his writing sucks and he's a hack.

But he knows there is no point in this race.

No matter how well he does, there is always someone who does better. Ranking is a snapshot in time, and while he can see his own ranking at all times, the people around him can't, and who these people are changes all the time. Another writer may have had a successful release or a big mailing list, and this is why their book suddenly surged past Jack's. Or they may have had a successful ad campaign.

He don't know what goes on in these writers' lives, and therefore it's pointless to worry about it. The only one who worries is him. He shouldn't seek approval from those writers who disapproved of his step to self-publish. He will never get it, even if deep in their hearts they're jealous that he was able to give up his job and they're still struggling to make more than a few hundred dollars per year.

It's not about them. It's about him.

He finally shuts down the computer and watches a movie with Tony.

ELEVEN

Marketing That's Right for You

TOM STARTED ASKING in the author Facebook group about marketing. Soon, it was clear to him that the other group members thought his questions ranged from ignorant to clueless. Never having done any marketing, he was just not familiar with the lingo.

A lot of people jumped on him with suggestions even he could see were out of his league. When he said so, a helpful person in the group said that older writers needed simpler solutions because they couldn't be expected to be up to speed with all the technology. Tom replied that he was happy to face her off in the use of mathematical software any time. And then Emily jumped in to defend Tom, because she felt just as clueless and she was young, and it was absolutely unfair to make the judgement that old equals technologically challenged. It almost broke out into a flame war.

Isn't the internet wonderful?

Fortunately, one of the moderators came up with the idea for the group to tailor marketing plans to specific writers. First, the group went about determining all the different types of marketing. Tom copies everything he learns into a single document:

YOUR BOOK'S LISTING: *passive marketing*

The best marketing starts with the book. If you don't have a book that looks attractive to the readers, they won't buy it.

Marketing starts with your book cover. Make sure it stands out, and make sure it communicates the genre and tone of the book.

Marketing is simply presenting your book in places where people are able to buy it.

This means that your listing at retailer sites is a form of marketing. More retailers equals more marketing.

It means that having your book in your email signature is a form of marketing. Even having an image in the header of your Facebook page that shows all your books is a form of marketing.

You want people to be familiar with what your book looks like so that when they feel like something new to read, and they happen to come across your book, they will be happy to give it a go.

You will want other writers to be familiar with your books, so that when they have a lull in their publishing schedule, they might be able to suggest that their readers try your books.

You want to make sure that when a reader gets to the end of your book, they find a link on what you want them to do next. In most cases this will be to buy the next book.

These are all very important tools for marketing your book. All of them are passive ways of marketing and every author should do them.

By this point you haven't spent a cent on ad sites. It is entirely possible to do successful marketing without buying a single ad.

Free books: passive marketing

Free books are an excellent way of advertising your catalogue. If you have written a number of books, make sure that you use a permafree book at least some of the time.

Much has been said recently about the supposed effectiveness of free books. People are saying it doesn't work any more, and that the readers are just freebie seekers and only want books for free. People will say that we're training readers that all books should be free and devaluing fiction.

But how is that going to work, when all you ever make free is your first book, it ends in a cliffhanger, and there are two more books in your series?

The people who want to read the rest of the series will buy the other books.

This is a form of advertising that doesn't cost you anything, but you will need to put some effort into it

You can just make your book free on all retailers, sit back and do nothing.

At first you get a number of downloads, but this starts to peter off very quickly.

You have to advertise.

You can do this by entering promotions, by buying ads, most specifically on the list sites like Freebooksy, or you can use pay-per-click ads, and some people have been using these to great effect. You can also cross-promote free books of other authors (and they promote yours).

Free book bundles

It can be quite effective to bundle your first-in-series free book with a number of other free books from other authors and make it a box set. These big bundles get more attention, because they represent great value to the reader, and a number of authors work together to promote the title.

It also has the effect of populating the strip of also-boughts on your book pages with the books by those other authors (and vice-versa), in which case you will be linked for more free cross-promotion. If one author in the collection has a successful release, everyone else benefits. It goes without saying that you need to carefully select the other authors. These opportunities exist in closed-door Facebook groups and amongst groups of friends. If you can't find a bundle to join, start your own. Get a couple of authors with similar books, get a nice cover and join all the books into a collection with Vellum (Tom makes a note: find out what Vellum is, because like a true geek, he hand-codes his own books, but doesn't know where to start with bundles). Upload and make it free everywhere. Then ask all participating authors to post to their audience staggered across the first few weeks. Buy some ads. Put it on Facebook and ask people to repost it.

Social media

You should set up an author page, and post there regularly. You can also get your fellow authors to like and share your posts. The constant struggle with many social media outlets is visibility. It will be reduced unless you get engagement on your posts. Learn to use hashtags for searchability.

Posting in Facebook promotional groups is generally pointless. Most of those groups are filled with authors. However some people have found limited success advertising free books there. It doesn't cost anything, so why not?

There may be better uses of your time.

Rented lists

These are websites that send links to free and discounted books to subscribers, where authors can pay an amount and have their books advertised to the site's audience.

The cost of taking part in these can range from free to a small amount of ten or fifteen dollars to hundreds. The cost will depend on the size of their list and the site's reputation.

The effect of a listing is limited to the day that the ad runs. But if you advertise the first book in a series, it's highly likely you will get further sales at a later stage.

Other than the limited duration, the disadvantages of using these lists repeatedly are that you can wear out the audience, that many of them aren't hugely effective, and that it may take quite a lot of time to keep making submissions.

Pay-per-click advertising

If you want to try pay-per-click advertising, it's probably a good idea to read up on it thoroughly before jumping in. It's possible to blow through a lot of money with not much to show for it. Sites like Facebook will eat your money very quickly if you give them half a chance.

You need to start conservatively and learn how to use the platform, where your audience is on it, and which are the most effective ad types.

Most of the courses and books mention that it is likely to cost some money before you have worked this out.

If you are not prepared to spend this money or time, you're better off not embarking on this type of advertising at all.

TOM DOESN'T LIKE SPENDING money, so he probably thinks this is not a good fit for him.

But someone suggests that he might be able to set up a couple of ads for very low budgets that keep running continuously. If he checks on the ads every few days, they can keep things ticking at a low level for a long time.

On Amazon, you will have to advertise a book, but on Facebook, you can advertise whatever you please. Some people suggest advertising free series starter books for people willing to sign up for an author mailing list. There are many different ways of using Facebook ads. Direct book sales is only one of them.

Pay-per-click advertising is a game of percentages. You don't earn big until you spend big.

Yeah, Tom is not sure that he has either the will or energy to do that right now.

In the end, Tom concludes that he should start with the passive advertising: make sure that his books are presented in the best possible way, and set up a mailing list (and actually use the list!) and optimise listings across all retailers. He can also see himself getting together with a group of authors to do something together. He might be able to find another author who has this magical Vellum thing.

Emily looks at Tom's document with a sense of dread, but if she really thinks about it, she can see herself buying some regular ads for her KDP Select free days (she should actually start using those!)

Jack and Lucy already do quite a lot of advertising, but they may still benefit from a regular re-jig to consider whether their current methods are still the best.

Since Jack was worried about the rising costs of pay-per-click advertising, he should probably change his strategy. Some of his audience may have shifted, or he might have burned them out.

Lucy might once have been happy with a lot of direct communication with her fans in Facebook groups, but she is feeling a bit vulnerable and fears that her books are being made a target. Maybe she can get some peace of mind with some simple paid ads.

TWELVE

Social Media: Do You Have To?

ON HEARING "SOCIAL MEDIA", Emily's courage sinks.

Not so long ago, she was searching for information about marketing online and she found an article that gave reasons why authors should have a Facebook page, and post something on the page every day, and "like" replies, because if you didn't do that, no one was going to see your posts.

And you had to be chatty and not talk about your books all the time.

It sounded all very sensible. After all, platforms like Facebook want their users to talk to each other, not be bombarded with quasi-ads.

But Emily doesn't "do" chatty, and she hates the idea of schmoozing fans because it's not her style

The words social media are the subject of dread for her. She is an introvert, and the idea of selling herself on a platform where everyone can see it strikes fear into her heart.

She sees other writers go all out on social media. They download lists of must-dos on social media, and follow them religiously. Tweet ten times a day, make two posts on Facebook, upload pictures of your book covers on Instagram, make boards for your books on Pinterest, and so on and so forth.

But do you know what?

None of it looks genuine. They're following a script, a checklist of things to do, that has been developed with someone else for a different purpose. Maybe the person who developed this list was a non-fiction author, or maybe the originator of the list was a marketing teacher who merely rattled off things you could try, and other people took the list as a must-do scenario.

Emily can never see this working for an author of fiction.

The people who developed those lists are not authors of fiction. They're people who sell courses on how to sell books. They like giving lists of actionable advice. The part of the advice that says, "Try these things," gets lost in translation.

They will say that you must be on Facebook or you must be active on Twitter, because that is important to them as a marketer of courses for authors.

So what should Emily really do?

Was it really necessary to do all that stuff?

Another romance writer, someone Emily respects a lot, says:

The thing that marketers forget about social media . . .

Is the word "social".

Social media has taken the position of the phone and letters as a way people communicate with each other. It's taken the position of magazines as a way to connect with people who share similar interests.

In some cases, you can sell things to these people, but the social aspect always comes first. It must be real, and it must be genuine. If it's not, it's better to make sure people understand that it's advertising: buy an ad.

If you feel forced when posting updates on Facebook and Twitter, you are never going to sound genuine. Not only that, but nobody is going to want to follow you, because your updates read like automated garbage, and people are on social media to interact.

So if you consider which social media platforms you should be on, consider first which ones you want to be on. These are most likely the ones that you're on already and the ones you use as a social being.

If your answer is: I hate social media, then don't. Simple as that. It's all about your fiction anyway. If people want to buy it, they'll buy it because they want to read it, not because you bombarded them with spam on social media.

So, Emily wants to know, I don't have to do social media at all? Her sigh of relief is almost audible.

It's not quite that easy, people in the group say. Because readers will still look for you on social media, and if you're not going to be present there, where do you want them to find you?

Emily says: Um—how about only on Amazon?

Sure, an experienced writer tells her, but I heard you say you were unhappy with the direction your sales were taking. You have to do something.

Yes, she has to do something.

But Emily is quite certain that being active on social media is not going to be it. On the other hand, she can see that readers who like her books would want to know when the next book is going to be out, and they want to find this out from her. She puts "set up website, mailing list and Facebook page" on her to-do list.

LUCY IS DOING social media very well. She runs a number of very active Facebook groups. One of those is for her animal protection interest.

The other is a group of readers whom she has befriended over the years she's been writing. They include her beta readers and her most ardent fans. This group can only be accessed from the back of her books, and every time she has a new idea or she's starting on a new book she talks to her readers about it. The group is active and friendly.

If you're reading this book in some unimaginable future where Facebook no longer exists, don't worry, because something else will have replaced it. We humans like to talk to each other, and we will always find ways to do so.

In the author group discussion, Lucy attributes much of her success to her reader group.

But, Tom asks, is Lucy marketing on Facebook?

It's true that her group of fans rushes out to buy her new book as soon as she publishes it. But she has not courted these people to be part of this group with the intent of selling to them. She runs the group as a service to her fans.

At this point, Jack gets a bit annoyed with Tom. Didn't he just read through the entire discussion where people outlined all the different kinds of active and passive marketing? Of course keeping up with your fans is marketing. Marketing is not just buying ads that you spray into the ether in a hopefully somewhat targeted way.

But the discussion circles back to Lucy's huge commitment to Facebook groups.

The focus of the second group she runs is very broad, and she doesn't mention her fiction often, although many people there will realise that she is an author and that her fiction represents her views on the subject.

The people in this group are a completely separate audience from her readers.

Well, that's not rocket science, you might say, and Lucy completely agrees with that.

But an author comes up with an example of another author who established a Facebook community about learning to write well. It became very popular, but the author was disappointed that the members of the group then didn't go on to buy his fiction. The question he raised was: Can an author establish a community around anything other than variations of "buy my book" for people who will actually, you know, buy the books? And if not, why should writers start or take part in these communities?

It's about paying it forward, Lucy says. You can certainly sell to these people, but their primary interest is going to be the reason they joined the group. They want to be better writers, they want to market their own books, they want to know about this particular period in history or, in my case, they care about the well-being of animals. In short, they are not there because they want to read my books.

It's pretty hard to find an interest group where the population of people who join are directly related to your fiction. People don't like being marketed to on social media, except when it's clearly an ad, and many people don't even like those. They're on social media to be social. We all know Facebook groups or Twitter hashtags that have been completely ruined by book spammers.

The only place where I can put up promotional material about my own fiction (and even then not all the time) is the group of fans I've built up who are there specifically for this reason. And at this point we circle back to the quality of and engagement with your fiction. Such fans are there because they read and liked your books.

In other words, trying to collect a huge social media following and expecting to sell to them before people have become fans of your fiction is putting the cart before the horse. And because, although the horse may be willing to push the cart, it will still require you to do a lot of steering and pulling to make sure it goes in the right direction. There are much better ways of doing this.

Be on social media because you like it. And if you don't, then don't.

Lucy admits to being an extrovert who is happiest when talking to other people, organising and directing stuff.

SO, what is it that we can or should do on social media?

Apart from Lucy, none of our other writers have a huge presence on social media. Tom distrusts Facebook, but he likes Twitter because he follows the news there. Emily forgot that she already has a Facebook page for her fiction, which is indicative of how much she posts there. Jack has a Facebook page (because you need one to advertise on Facebook), but also doesn't do much there.

As self-professed haters of social media, what should Tom and Emily do about it?

Jack says:

Think about it from the perspective of a reader who has enjoyed your books. They may not be willing to sign up for a mailing list (because many people don't), but they still want to know when the next book is out. Of course they can sign up on Amazon, but not everyone buys there, or Bookbub, but not everyone even knows what that is. The Facebook site has pretty good SEO, so when a random reader types in your name (providing it's not John Smith) or your name and the title of your book, the sites that will come up are: your website (if you have a self-hosted one where your name is in the URL or title), Amazon (but they don't want that, because they already bought the book) and Facebook, if you have a page there, and/or Twitter, if you have an account where your name is in the bio.

So even if you never plan to do anything on these sites, at the very least open an account, make a Facebook page and make sure that your first post and/or bio mentions where people can contact you instead. Do the same at all major social media outlets.

It costs nothing.

And when Emily goes to her neglected Facebook page, she finds, to her great embarrassment, that readers have been trying to contact her there. One message is from a mother who tells her that her sixteen-year-old daughter went missing six months ago, and she found a copy of Emily's paranormal romance books on her desk in her room, tied with a pink ribbon, so she must have been enjoying them very much.

Now Emily feels extremely embarrassed.

Writing is not the one-way street she has been acting like it is. Your writing affects people, and you owe it to those people to give them an outlet to contact you, and also to respond to them.

She adds to her list: Talk to at least one fan every day.

THIRTEEN

You Must Write More Books

Throughout the lifetime of the author group, there is one piece of advice that keeps coming back: if you want success, you must write more books.

Tom wants to know: How many, and is that always the answer?

Yes, it's a loaded question, because he doesn't really feel like writing more books that won't sell, and ever since Helena's health took a turn for the worse, he's spending a lot of time in the hospital. Frankly his mind isn't in the right place to spend so much time on something he isn't even sure will sell.

So he asks the question, but what he really wants to hear is: No, you don't need to write more books. You can fix the ones you have.

But the group crushes that thought pretty quickly. It's almost always true that more books is better, until it isn't.

When is it true?

In general, if you have few books, if you have series that are selling reasonably well, if you have a plan to use book 1 in a series in a giveaway or a free box set, or give it to subscribers to your mailing list, you should write more books as quickly as you can.

It's also true if you want to try another series, another pen name or a slightly different genre.

It is not true when you already have a lot of books and each new book you write does little to increase your overall income, or when you're sick of a series and hate the thought of it.

Tom says that the release of his last book did little to increase his income, and one of the group's bestselling authors came back pretty hard on this: Tom, mate, you have only four books. That's not a lot. The first three sold reasonably well, so the seed of something good is clearly there. The fourth book doesn't sell, because the cover says Book 1. Where is Book 2?

Emily is quiet during this discussion. She realises that she's running on the escalators in the wrong direction, putting out more and more books, while her overall income is staying the same at best.

So in her case, it's not so much about *more* books, it's about *what kind* of books will get her out of the rut. She wants books that keep selling for longer.

Jack says that the major difference between Tom and Emily is that Emily's books kind of accidentally discovered a market, and Tom's didn't.

But clearly the market is shifting away from the type of books Emily writes. She hasn't spent any time learning about her audience, and has no mailing list to speak of, so she has to start over from the very bottom. That is dispiriting and a shame, because Emily's books were well loved by the readers, if only she could follow to where these readers are.

Writing more books with more of the same isn't going to help

Emily. She should step back and figure out a new direction, but writing more books will help Tom.

And with this remark, Jack again puts his foot into it. He's just so good at diagnosing other people's issues without ever following up on his own advice.

Let's look at Jack.

FOURTEEN

Completing Things

THE BEST WAY TO DESCRIBE Jack's catalogue of books is "scattershot". He's written in a few genres, has some standalone work and unfinished series.

He's been pretty much like that all his life: flitting from one thing to the next. Jack of all trades, master of none.

Because he tends to shoot off at the mouth in the author group, he only has a few people he can trust with the truth. The best-selling author who started the group, Luke, is one of them.

Luke says: Look, mate, it is hard to decide whether to continue something that's not doing well, but what does this say to readers? It says: this dude never finishes anything. Don't bother waiting for the next volume. In fact, why should they bother at all?

Luke is not known to mince his words.

Jack finds it hard to pick which series he should continue. He enjoys writing one series much more than the other, but it sells less and it's not as clear-cut in the genre.

Luke says: Leaving series unfinished looks untidy and scattershot.

We all know the one or two authors who never seem to be able to finish anything. With every new volume of their series they dig themselves deeper into a hole from which it seems to be almost impossible to come to a satisfactory conclusion.

Planning and finishing a series is a skill. You're not a beginning writer, and you should have the skill set to finish what you started.

But Jack thinks: Except I don't.

He says that he's not sure series work well in his genre anyway.

Luke says: Which genre? You've written in four that I can see.

Yeah. That's right.

To make matters worse, Jack's had some other ideas. He wants to start on them, because, hey, shiny new idea! He could just take "Book 1" off the cover of his first books, but for at least one of those books, the ending makes it very clear that another book is planned. Jack confides that he's just not very good at this branding and series thing.

Luke writes out a long post about his approach to series, here paraphrased by Tom:

Starting a series

When you realise that a story is going to develop into a series, plan a number of exit points, at which you can rest or even abandon the series. The first exit point could be at the end of book 1, which means that book 1 is a standalone book with series potential. Plan other exit points at book 3 and 4 and 5.

If you really wanted to be meta, you could write three standalone book 1s and see which one sold best to decide which series you should complete.

People advocate dropping a series once the sales are lower than a predetermined number.

While that all sounds very businesslike and analytical, Luke thinks this is a dumb move for a number of reasons, especially for early-career writers who don't have a huge stable of finished series yet:

- Up until about three or four books, a series will generate more income when you add books.
- A completed series is a valuable advertising asset.
- There is no guarantee that a new series will sell any better. It may not, and then you have just discarded a lot of work for nothing.
- You can't control how well a series will sell. You can control how well you advertise it (Jack understands advertising). Advertising is where you make money, but you need more books than one, and preferably, the series needs to be completed, or at least have three books, before you can do too much with it. So finish it and then we go and make some money with that puppy.

So Luke would never discontinue a series?

He would and he has, but only if the sell-through is really poor. He writes fantasy and doesn't worry terribly much about the sell-through between book 1 and 2. After all, you're going to advertise the living daylights out of book 1, and might give it away for free. Lots of people are going to get the book who have no intention of reading it. We know that free books languish on a lot of Kindles, and we're not going worry about the books that aren't read. We worry about the ones that are.

But if the sell-through between book 2 and 3 is poor, Luke says he definitely wouldn't write any more books. That's great, because he planned an exit point at book 3 anyway.

What is poor sell-through?

By the time you get to the end of book 2 in a series, people should be hooked. At this stage, you should see sell-through percentages of over 80%. If your series sell-through from book 2 to 3 is 50%, can it after book 3. Because by the time you get to book 4, you've lost too many people and making a profit on your ads becomes increasingly harder.

But that doesn't mean you should discard the series. It's worth more if your sell-through is higher, so you might want to see if you can do something about that first.

Have a look at the reviews of book 2. Do they state a couple of clear issues why people don't read on after book 2? If so, you might want to employ a beta reader and ask them to look at the book with those comments in mind. And then, if possible, fix them.

Let's make money with this puppy!

A completed series of three books is an asset that you can use to create more sales. When you hold a sale on the first book, or give the first book away for free, a certain percentage of people will buy the other books. The more books you sell cheaply or give away, the more you will sell. The numbers may not be stellar, but as long as your sell-through is good, add them up over time and your series becomes a constant source of income.

It could be that the first book responds quite well to pay-per-click advertising, or that when given the book for free, quite a high percentage of people enjoy it and are prepared to pay for the next books. The success of the first book in the series when you first launched it doesn't always align with the sell-through to the rest of the series. You can use a series with a high sell-through rate to great effect, even if book 1 never sold terribly well on its own.

But you can't do this as effectively when the series doesn't at least have three books in total and the ending is left hanging.

Series design

Planning a series is no different from planning a novel, except on a larger scale. Except now you would expand the story's sections or chapters into individual volumes. Each of the volumes needs to tell a separate story. If the volumes are more open-ended, keep the release of all volumes tight, or release all the books at the same time.

Luke says he tends to plan series in lots of three. This is not because he thinks that by three books you should be able to tell whether or not a series is going to be a bestseller. You can probably tell this by the first book.

You can't plan for fluke bestsellers, but you can plan for a three-part asset that you'll use to generate a steady income.

How do you design a series?

There are several ways. You can make it so that each volume tells its own story and the books can be read in any order, or so the books follow one another and can't stand alone.

The first requires a protagonist who never changes and who faces a different, unrelated, problem each time. Examples of this format are the famous detective series where the focus is on solving the crime, and developments in the life of the main characters are non-existent.

Most series need to be read in some sort of order because, even if they deal with individual issues, there is a larger story arc, even if it's only that the main characters learn and age.

Then there is the trilogy.

A lot of antagonism exists in the author community against series that are "just a very big story chopped into three parts", but it's very common in fantasy.

You know one of the most famous books that did just that?

It's called *The Lord of the Rings*.

Yeah. That.

If you happen to write fantasy, as Luke does, planning a very large story and dividing it into three sections is a very good way of designing a series that will both earn you money and is easy to abandon once you decide it didn't work as well as you hoped. After all, it's done after three books.

If it sold well, then you can decide to write more books. If you weren't happy with sales, then it's still a completed series that you can use in advertising.

If you write a series, you should look ahead. Keep a notebook with the major events you are going to cover in each volume and how they are going to end. It is best if you cover a distinct event in each volume. If you have a large story arc that needs to be completed, make sure you plan where you are going from the beginning. Start with a story arc spanning three books. Plan for a further story arc that could take the series to five or six books. Make sure that after three books enough plot threads have been resolved that you can leave the series if necessary.

THAT'S EASIER SAID than done, however. Jack thanks Luke for this and contemplates his mess of books. His most popular series has two books. Writing the third book in the series, which readers are forever asking him to do, might be the easiest option.

With a few of the other books, he might get away with taking "Book 1" off the cover. He does know how to do graphic design.

While he's at it, he might change a few of the covers so that it's clear the books are all by the same author. That's the next best thing to having a completed series.

FIFTEEN

Time Management

LUCY IS WORRIED about her upcoming release. If only she could find some extra time.

She asks in the group: how do you guys manage to find time to write?

Tom has recently bought a tablet so that he can take it when he goes with his wife to her health appointments. He often writes in little snatches of time. He's not employed full-time, but he might as well have a job.

Jack works at home. He tries to write for an hour every morning after he's gone for a run. The rest of the day is taken up with marketing activities until his partner comes home.

Emily lives alone. She chose to get a cat instead of a dog, because she doesn't have to walk it. Emily has lots of time. The question is spending it wisely.

Lucy has two children. They go to school, so the day is free, but on weekends, they need to go to soccer and drama, and her husband won't do any of this.

When Lucy is not doing the team's snack duty, she goes for a walk. (*Psst!* Don't tell her husband that the soccer game was not that far away and she could have come home while her son was playing.) She's uses her phone to dictate a chapter or two.

Jack posts a link in the group to a talk about this subject. This is the gist of it:

Writers talk about the troubles finding the time to write, especially those who are just beginning.

This is a big subject with some people, as if they expect there to be an easy fix.

For some people, there isn't one solution. They have other commitments that they can't or don't want to drop. They might enjoy the day job. They may not make enough money from their writing to quit the day job yet. They may be looking after relatives, either small children or elderly parents, who require varying amounts of attention.

Time management is never going to be easy, because no matter how much you talk about it there are only twenty-four hours in the day. If you take up one thing, the flipside is that you must spend less time on another thing.

If you have a day job, you are quite lucky. Most likely, your job will involve time spent getting to and from work. A commute in a train or bus can be ideal for getting some words in. You will also have the necessary finances to buy equipment to allow you to do this. You can write on your phone with the aid of Scrivener for iOS. You can use dictation while walking, or get an iPad to take places where you may need to wait for a while, such as watching kids at swimming.

If you have a day job, you are also reasonably likely to be blessed with something called lunchtime.

This is a luxury to some of us, especially those with small children.

Many day jobs are highly structured, which allows you to structure your writing around them. You get to work at the same time, you have lunch at the same time, you leave at the same time, and spend roughly the same amount of time getting there. This allows you many different snippets of your day where, given the right mind frame and technology, you can get some words in. Even if you only write 100 extra words a day this could amount to one novel in a year.

That is, assuming that all you ever get to write is 100 words on the bus.

If you're caring for relatives, it's going to be much harder, because often the nature of your other activities is going to be erratic, and you need to be able to put things away at the drop of a hat.

In this case, having something with you where you can write in the little snatches of time you do get is very valuable. Again the trick is training yourself to think in small snippets of time and in paragraphs.

The writers discuss it in the group, and this is the summary of their conclusions:

News flash: it is very hard to stay focused for long stretches of time on a daily basis anyway. There are only very few writers who can do this successfully for long stretches of time.

As a writer whose primary activity during the day is not writing, you have a certain advantage. You learn to focus very clearly from the word go.

If you have little time, your time must be wisely spent. You will know that the most important thing you can do is to write more fiction.

You probably feel that other people are writing far more fiction than you, and that you could write so much if only you had the time.

You will probably spend less time marketing, and therefore probably waste less time on it.

You day job gives you things to write about. Hate your colleague? Make him a villain. Going on a work trip? Raunchy Christmas party? Use them in your fiction.

If you're caring for someone, it is highly likely that this situation is temporary. Kids grow up, elderly folk unfortunately die, and it is best to spend as much time with either as you can. It's not going to last forever.

Quite often, the fiction of people who have cared for a relative can be very emotional or full of black humour. You can use this to great effect. Recognise that your situation is not the same as everyone else's. Make sure that you differentiate yourself according to the experience that you have. If you're a writer, but you also have an interesting job, you will bring something to your fiction that a full-time writer doesn't have. If you are caring for relatives you will understand things that many writers won't. You will know how to connect with people in similar situations, and there are many of those.

If you're a student, you're probably studying with the aim of getting a degree and a better job. In that case, studying should probably be your first priority (especially if your parents are paying for it!).

Most of these interruptions are temporary in nature. Examine your priorities and act accordingly. Next year, the situation may be very different.

If, however, you have the tendency to fritter away time on Facebook or slump in front of the television at night or lose hours in gaming, you may need to restructure your day if you want to get anything done.

Time spent at home not doing anything that you absolutely need to do is time you could spend writing.

So carve out one hour a day—it could be in the morning, if you're a morning person, or it could be after dinner or just before going to bed. Whatever takes your fancy, take that hour, and make sure there are no interruptions. Make sure that the children are in bed and that your adult relatives understand that this is your writing time.

If you have small children, putting on a movie is a great thing.

If you have a large and boisterous family and live in a small apartment, you may need to learn to become less insistent on silence while writing. Learning to write anywhere and shutting yourself off from distractions is a skill we can all learn.

In the end it is all about how badly you want it.

If you can't come up with any time to write, you may not want it badly enough. If your job is so busy that you don't have any time whatsoever, you're probably quite well paid. You may be able to take an extended period of leave to write a book or two.

You may need to look for a different job.

How badly do you want it? Make sure that your excuse of not having time is genuine and that you're not looking for an excuse to do nothing.

SIXTEEN

Focus On Story

TOM MAKES A DECISION.

At this time, he neither has the will or energy to write book 2 of the series that didn't sell.

He's been told his first series sold better than average, so maybe he can make it better. Some of the comments from group members have gotten under his skin, especially the ones suggesting that his style was quaint and old and the insinuation that this is to be expected from an old author. Just the previous day, someone in the hospital called Helena, at 61, "quite young". He's not ready to face the scrap heap. Or if that's his lot, he's going to go down fighting.

So he writes to one of the bestselling authors in the group, and true to the spirit of the community, the author, whose name is Luke, engages Tom in a pretty comprehensive discussion. Here is the gist of it:

Story alignment issues

Tom wrote from his heart. He wrote the type of fiction that he might have been reading thirty years ago. Surprise, surprise—in the meantime the world has changed. There is probably still an audience for his stories, an audience which looks much like him, but it's likely that the audience is quite small and easily exhausted. Also, like himself, they are probably quite cynical about things like advertising, and prefer to stick to the classics in the genre.

Tom needs to focus on his content. He needs to look at the way of modern storytelling and align his fiction with the tastes of modern readers. You remember how Tom said that he didn't like much of the fiction in this current genre?

Oh dear.

This presents a problem indeed.

The fact that he wrote a book like those that were famous thirty years ago or more doesn't necessarily mean that new readers will enjoy his fiction as much as earlier generations did. The type of fiction may not be very popular any more and may not have aged well. It's likely that the type of fiction still exists, but Tom needs to go and find where it hangs out, and what the new tropes are.

But, Tom says, people still read the old classics. I don't see why I can't write like that.

Totally, he can, but he was complaining about sales, right?

Luke says that the bottom line is that he is not one of those famous authors that he thought to emulate. Readers these days are attracted by different elements in their fiction.

Tom has a choice: he can adapt his fiction, or he can adapt his expectations. Or, before he does any of this, he can try some advertising, but he's already said he doesn't like running ads and he's pretty emotionally tied up with his wife's illness right now, so Luke won't suggest that to him.

Tom grumbles a bit that fiction now is supposed to be more politically correct, whatever that is supposed to mean. Maybe in this case it means: I'm an old fogey who can't be bothered to find out what audiences these days like. Maybe it means: I can't even be bothered to find out who I'd like to read my books, other than "people like me and people I want to be like me".

Luke says: Mate, that is a valid audience, but if it doesn't turn out to be very large, and you want to sell better, something needs to give.

Story structure issues

Luke then goes on to say that Tom's way of storytelling is slightly stale.

Not just the subject matter and presentation of fiction changes over time. Also the style of storytelling has changed.

When people didn't have much option to watch movies in the genre, a lot of the scenery needed to be described in exquisite detail. You rarely see this in fiction any more. People tend to get bored by it. You don't have to tell anyone what Paris looks like. A lot of readers will have been there themselves.

Modern audiences are far less tolerant of wooden characters, long sections of description, dialogue that exists only to show a certain plot point, or fiction that is unnecessarily emotionally distant.

Readers want to connect with a character who is engaging, possibly sympathetic, and definitely takes an active role in the story and has an interesting personal story to tell.

Many of the older books, especially in the traditionally male genres, were quite distant. They were about the plot much more than about the characters. They were about nifty ideas and clever plot twists.

It's not just the characterisation that has changed.

The style of storytelling has changed on a sentence level.

Stories in a lot of genre fiction are told in a tight prose, with few flowery passages or clever turns of phrase. It could be that Tom's writing and interests align more closely with literary fiction.

If this is so, and he wants to go in that direction, he would also have to adjust his expectations. Literary fiction can sell quite well, but it is harder to sell, and harder to market. For one, you are competing with a lot of very well-known writers who are backed by the big publishers.

TOM SAYS: So, basically, my writing sucks?

Luke replies:

If you want to see it that way, it's up to you. I'm only saying that in order to sell better, something needs to change. Your style and subject matter comes across to me as old-fashioned. That's where I'd start to make changes.

You've already said you're not going to do big ad campaigns, and to be honest, I think that would be a waste of money. For those campaigns to be successful, you need to be a bit closer to the market, otherwise you'll just burn through your budget with that pretty cover. Man, those covers are really awesome. Who did them?

So Tom asks: What should I do?

Luke says: if you're prepared to do the work, I would find a developmental editor to see if you can work on style and story craft. Personally, I wouldn't touch your existing books, but write something new.

Except Tom only has his existing books.

SEVENTEEN

But You Will Kill Your Career!

MEANWHILE, LUCY IS still upset over that one-star review. Amazon won't take it down. The people in the author group tell her to ignore it, but then the same person gives another one-star review to another of her books. This is a fairly new book that doesn't have so many reviews, and it drops her average to 4 stars.

Again, the other writers tell her to ignore it, but she can't. This nasty person obviously has it in for her, and it's all her own fault.

She has been told numerous times that writers can't be involved in anything remotely political, but Lucy likes that sort of thing. Animal protection isn't related to writing, but it's just that it is causing her a tremendous amount of heartache.

Should she stop being political on social media?

She doesn't know who to ask about this. Her husband will probably just tell her to quit writing if it bothers her so much, and he would be happier for it. At least he—or the absence of him—would get her undivided attention.

Then she remembers Jack.

Jack is very different from her. He's so sure of himself, so good with his ads, he knows so much. But Jack is gay and he makes no secret of being gay. She is a Facebook friend of his, and he often reposts political pro-gay posts.

She asks him: Should I stop posting about animal rights?

Jack says (in the time he should be writing):

Writers are often advised that "it will kill your career" if you utter as much as a word that could be interpreted as political. I want to stop that sentiment in the bud.

There is nothing that will kill your career unless you stop writing.

We all know that famous writer who flies off the handle at reviewers who dare to post negative reviews on her books. We know the old fogey writer who insists that the best place for women is in the kitchen. We know the literary writer who delights in rubbishing every other writer, especially those of genre fiction.

We know the writer who is generally a dick online all around.

People say they won't read these writers anymore, and indeed some people don't.

But many more people won't even know that this is going on. They're not in the places where these people have misbehaved or sprouted their unpalatable political views. They're looking for a book to read.

So if being a general dick doesn't harm the career of famous writers who spend a fair amount of time in the spotlight, why should it harm you?

I'm not advocating that you should be a dick online, because there are other ways in which it may harm you, but in your sales, it won't.

Even if a huge online argument breaks out, the collective memory of the internet is about twenty-four hours and after that, everyone has moved on and the vast majority of people can't even remember the name of the writer who said all these stupid things online. Never mind the things that were highly partisan but by no means stupid, or the writers who simply said something of a political nature.

Being political does NOT hurt your sales. In fact, it can attract people of a similar bent, and those who don't share your view probably wouldn't have enjoyed your fiction anyway.

Saying something stupid online, or getting into a public argument also does NOT harm your career.

The only thing that will harm your career is if you stop writing.

Lucy has no intention of doing that, although she very much doubts that her new book is going to be well received. It's about a woman who rescues dogs. It will probably give the trolls more ammunition to one-star her.

Jack goes on: That said, being a dick online will absolutely harm the opportunities other writers are willing to give you. If you're known to be hard to work with, this will go around to the organisers of promotions, to the owners of promotion sites, to the people looking for others to include in box sets.

Lucy says: I know that. I organise those sets. Some people are just horrible to work with.

Jack says: I didn't know that. You should advertise in the group. You might get some interest from other writers.

Lucy thinks: If only I were as self-assured and confident as you are.

EIGHTEEN

You Have To Be Professional

WHEN EMILY FIRST STARTED WRITING, she didn't have two cents to rub together. It was just after her divorce and she couldn't afford any of the things that the well-meaning "they" said she should have. Yet she feels that those books she wrote back then, edited with the help of a friend and published with a —really substandard—cover she cobbled together herself, take a place in her career that will never be replaced by any other book with the slick production she has now. She has of course paid to edit those books and has put nice covers on them, but there is something about the raw emotion in those stories that captured a lot of readers despite the amateur presentation that she's having trouble reproducing in her other books.

She's questioning the whole mantra of slick professionalism.

There is such thing as spending too much money on books.

Tom knows better than most that there is a tremendous pressure in the self-publishing industry for writers to spend big on their books before they have earned the first dollar in sales. He's had a fair few people knock on his virtual door.

This is what a veteran writer said about it:

The advice goes that you have to invest if you want to be in business.

If you start a shop, that would be true. You would have to buy stock, you would have to refurbish the shop-front that you just signed an expensive lease for, and you would have to invest in employing someone even if it's only to do your accounts.

Starting like a writer does not need to be like that. It is in fact one of the beauties of the business.

Self-publishing is a very democratic movement. Anyone with an internet account and text editor can do it. You can make use of free resources to clean up your book and create a cover.

No, it wouldn't look "professional", but there is nothing to stop you doing this, to check out if a project has legs before you invest more money into it.

For people who aren't sure if they want to do this writing gig, or people who don't have a lot of money to spend, the bootstrapping method is awesome, because another basic tenet of business, apart from having to invest funds in your business for it to be successful, is never to spend more than you earn.

In the beginning of someone's self-publishing career these two things are diametrically opposed.

On the one hand we have bestseller writers pressuring new writers to spend big on the covers and their editing, and on the other hand we have people who advise writers to work their way up and upgrade from the proceeds of sales.

I am quite wary of writers who advise others to get professional straight off the bat.

I don't see a problem with the actual advice. It is good advice. The cover does sell a book, and editing is extremely important. Both could make or break a book.

The problem lies in the fact that when you are new, you're unlikely to know how to pick a good cover, or good cover designer, or how to pick the right editor for you.

I have seen more than one writer spend thousands on a really beautiful cover that was totally inappropriate for the book, or made by an artist who had absolutely no clue about topography.

It just makes me sad to see this happen to people who have spent cash they probably couldn't lose and wasted it because they felt this great urge to "be professional".

As far as I'm concerned, bootstrapping your way to better covers and better editing is completely professional. Never spending more than you earn is utterly professional.

You only spend big whenever you can afford to gamble, or you are pretty sure that you are going to make that money back. Spend when you're a bit more experienced.

The advice that "you have to be professional" usually comes with a price tag for a product or service we should be willing to buy because "you have to be professional".

Jack agrees. He says he recently went through all his expenses and was quite horrified with the number of auto-renews coming out of his credit card for services he barely used. So he cancelled a few. So many of these services sell themselves with the promise that it's "only" $10 a month, but a handful of these subscriptions can really add up.

If you really want to be professional, you need to evaluate what you're spending and whether those services are still useful to you. Some of them will be worth it to you, absolutely.

"Being professional" is not about using the services or not, it's about evaluating whether you do, or would, get your money's worth out of them.

NINETEEN

Find New Audiences

EMILY HAS BEEN WORKING through her list of things to do. She made a note to check her Facebook page for messages once a day, and see if anything needs to be replied to.

She does eventually reply to the woman with the missing daughter, explaining that she's been in a difficult position herself. The woman writes back saying that she can understand. Emily is not sure she deserves forgiveness.

She also connected with a reader called Chris, who is also recently divorced and trying to find work while looking after a five-year-old girl.

Emily pays for a writer from the author group to set up a website and sets up a mailing list signup. She's dismayed that three people sign up on the first day, and five on the second day.

She also plans to use her **KDP** Select free days for the first time ever, and she books some promo sites to go with it.

But after doing that, she's stuck. What else is she supposed to be doing?

Jack seems to know a lot about advertising, so she asks him.

Jack says that because Emily wasn't doing any marketing, all her new books would have appealed to the same people. For marketing, she would have relied solely on the algorithms that kept recommending her books to other people on the retailer sites. These algorithms favour churn: new books, new authors, at an ever-increasing rate. This is especially true on Amazon, and Emily's books are all in Kindle Unlimited.

Her books might have fallen out of favour with the algorithms. It could have been because some programmer at 2 a.m. in the bowels of Amazon changed a line of code. It could have been because a new author launched a series of very successful books which took the recommendation slots Emily's books used to take up.

The pool of readers might have been on the move anyway, to another, new genre. She will never know.

Since writing more and more books is not going to be a solution for her, she probably needs to cut down on her writing and work out who her audience is and how to increase it.

There are several ways of doing this. If Emily doesn't already have a mailing list, she should start one, and start talking to those people. (She can respond with a tick on that one). She could look at the other books that retailers suggest people buy at the same time as buying hers. This will give her valuable information about where she can find an additional audience.

If she had an active Facebook page it would have valuable information on the location, age and other demographics of her audience. Unless she paid for Facebook likes, which she hasn't, this will represent a good section of her audience and their characteristics. Are they male or female, what country are they in, what age are they? With these characteristics, Emily can find authors who make a good target in advertising or who she can collaborate with. She might discover that her fiction is popular in certain countries. She could try to concentrate on those countries by selecting other people who have big audiences there and whose audience she can use.

But she has only twelve likes on her page.

Jack suggests that she should put her Facebook page in the back of all her books and ask her readers to "like" it.

Emily feels like she's finally starting to understand this. There is a lot more to having a website or Facebook page than meets the eye. It's not always about the blatantly commercial stuff you do there, says Jack, but if you engage people there, you can find out other things about them, such as which other writers they like. And that can be very helpful.

She doesn't need to write any new fiction for this, since she will be looking for new audiences who are not familiar with her fiction. She could try giving books away for free to the mailing list of other authors. She could set up swap requests with authors in those genres: she gets to mention books by other writers to her readers, and those writers will do the same for her.

Jack is pleased to hear that Emily has already set up a free promotion.

With the information about her audience and their popular books, Emily will be in a much better place to target future projects she wants to write.

TWENTY

Some Possibilities

A FEW DISCUSSIONS in the group are initiated by other people, and some apply to our writers.

Should you start a new genre?

In an ideal world, you should stick to a narrow brand and focus on its audience only.

But, as Emily has experienced, there are two risks attached to this.

The first is burnout. You just get too jaded, too tired of the same things. You run out of ideas and stories no longer feel fresh. You lose enthusiasm and your writing output and quality suffers.

The second risk, as Emily also experienced, is that the audience shifts elsewhere. This can happen quite abruptly, or very slowly over time.

Writing in another genre spreads the risk of this happening.

But beware of excessive fragmentation. This is a problem that Jack faces, which also means that he needs to spend such a lot on advertising, because the books in his catalogue don't neatly feed into each other. He's got little bits of unfinished series and incomplete catalogues floating about everywhere.

What he really needs to do is finish some of his unfinished stuff and tidy up some other unfinished series.

While he's working on that—and it's not a quick project—how can he mitigate the problems?

In the first place, by branding well. He should design all his covers in a similar style, for example, with a similar font for his name. While he's at it, he should get the cover designer to make him covers for the books that aren't yet written, but need to be written to complete the series. When Jack says he's a graphic artist, people wonder why he hasn't done this yet.

Good question.

If his branding is the same across all his books, readers will know that the books are written by him, and the image on the cover will help the readers understand which genre they are. He will need to have a strong website which lists all his books. He will need to have links to all his books in the back of each book. He will probably need to work his mailing list pretty extensively.

Multiple pen names

If you start another genre, should you be using another pen name?

Emily has toyed with the creation of new pen names but has pretty much abandoned it because it was too much work to keep all the profiles and "careers" of both writers alive.

Lucy has a successful pen name, and she publishes a book or two per year in that name. It's not a secret to her fan group that she has this name, but she uses it as a genre delineation. Her pen name books are more explicit in nature.

Jack started a new pen name when he started self-publishing in case any stigma from this activity tarnished his traditional publishing career. He then found there wasn't, so he merged everything under one name. Since he only used his initials instead of this first name, that was easy. (Tip: you can just change the name on a book as long as it's only an ebook without an ISBN. Once your book is in print, you need to publish a new version).

Whether to use a pen name will depend on a number of factors. In the first place, you want to make sure you do it for the right reasons. If your pen name is to experiment with a new genre and that genre is very much unlike your current genre and attracts audiences that are incompatible with your current genre, it is probably a good idea to start another pen name.

Examples often cited are children's book authors writing racy fiction, or distinguishing between fiction and non-fiction.

There are some genres where you may easily use the same pen name for both genres. Science Fiction and Fantasy are very much alike and unless you want to micro target your audience—and are prepared to do the additional work—there probably isn't much point or need for a new pen name. It just creates a lot of work for you.

If you write children's fiction and adult fiction, of the sexually explicit type, the situation is pretty clear-cut. And this highlights the reason why I think a pen name is useful: when the audiences for each genre are clearly separate.

Young children and adult readers are obviously very different people. If you write for children, you can't swear and a number of subjects won't interest them. But if you write crime and science fiction, the difference isn't going to be so great. Your readers are adults in both cases, and things like sex and swearing are going to be acceptable to both audiences in the same amount. If your science fiction is of the mystery or crime-solving type, I can see no reason to separate out real world crime fiction under a new name.

Another way of subdividing your audiences is through their reading behaviour. You could have a pen name that is 100% in Kindle Unlimited, whereas fiction under another name is not.

Your pen name doesn't need to be a secret. It could merely be a shortcut for a different type of fiction.

However, having another pen name has the potential to create a lot of extra work.

What are you going to do about a mailing list, a website and social media presence for your pen name? If you don't want this to become onerous, you need to think carefully about how you're going to manage this.

Here are some things you can do to reduce the amount of work required:

- Keep the same mailing list and make it clear to your audience who the pen name is and what it's for.
- Separate the mailing list, but keep it under the same account and cross-pollinate both
- Forego a website and have a Facebook page only
- Use a secondary service, like Draft2Digital, to display your pen name books on a single page as you would on a website

TWENTY-ONE

Broaden Your Horizon

FOLLOWING HER DISCUSSION WITH JACK, Emily has a looked at some ad possibilities, including the Facebook ad portal, but it all feels foreign to her, and it feels like mastering it will take a long time.

She asks about this in the group: How soon can I see results from this?

The replies vary from "I faffed around and spent money for no return for a year before something clicked and the ads started working," to "They worked for me straight away." There were also people who'd spent a lot of money on ads without anything to show for it.

Then Tom said: I don't want to state the obvious, but why don't you take some of your books out of Kindle Unlimited?

To which some other writers replied that was a terrible idea, because the vast majority of books that sell well in Emily's cosy mystery genre are in Kindle Unlimited.

But Tom is adamant. He says: I'm in the same boat. My genre is all Kindle Unlimited. I have only three books that sell anything worth squat, and my sales are a few hundred a month. A bit over half those sales are not on Amazon. I know it's not much, but I don't do any marketing and the sales are pretty constant. With all the books you have, you should be able to make at least ten times what I get.

Emily likes the sound of that. She doesn't live expensively—the notion of having a lot of money is still novel to her—and has some reserve. Because she and her cat don't spend much, it's worth a try. She doesn't like being beholden to one retailer anyway.

But it's a lot of work. She now needs EPUB files of all her books, wants to update the back matter while she's at it—she needs to put her new mailing list signup there!—needs to open accounts at other retailers, decide which ones to go direct and which ones to access through an aggregator. Initially she thinks to just use an aggregator for everything, but Lucy points out, rightly, that their 10% cut can add up to quite a bit of money once you start selling well.

She sends Tom a private message to ask about any pitfalls she needs to consider.

Tom, thorough fellow that he is, has kept a check sheet for the publishing process on all retailers, and he sends Emily a copy.

It's amazing (note to the reader: if you want to know about this, read *Going Wide Unboxed*).

He says: If you have any questions, let me know. I'll reply tonight when I'm home from the hospital.

And then they talk a bit about Helena, who has gone into surgery, and Emily's dad who died of cancer last year.

In the middle of going through Tom's instructions, she gets a random email from a fan who asks her if she's ever thought of putting her books on Apple, and when Emily says "Guess what I'm doing?" the woman is very happy.

Meanwhile, Tom rushes home to get a new set of pyjamas for Helena when she wakes up out of her surgery, and he does the shopping. He talks to his daughter and then Helena's brother rings from Greece. Should he and his wife visit after Helena recovers? Implied is that it might well be the last time he will talk to his sister. So then there is the visit for Tom to arrange, beds to take down from the attic and put together in the spare bedroom.

And while he's doing all this, it dawns on him that when you go to the Amazon chart of science fiction, you will notice that almost everyone has their books in Kindle Unlimited. There is a bit of bias going on, because the charts favour books that are in Kindle Unlimited, but the fact remains that a number of science fiction writers do very well in the program.

Since Tom is not getting a lot of sales on his new series he might take book 1 down, then write the others and then release the lot quickly in Kindle Unlimited. He doesn't have much of an audience elsewhere, and there is much potential for growth for him. If his type of book is going to be popular, this will be where it's at. He can always later remove the books and place them wide. Right now, he doesn't have any mental space to think about this.

This is how he has come to see it: KU is an easy, short-term strategy that can be successful for launching series. However, it cannibalises more of your sales the longer you stay in it. Being wide is a long-term strategy that should probably be the long-term default for all books.

TWENTY-TWO

Sacrifices and Family

ONE DAY, UNANNOUNCED, Lucy's husband comes home early from work. He's never early, so it's clear that something is up.

He says that they had a work meeting, that there will be changes in the company and management wanted to give older workers a chance to step out by offering them packages.

They explained everything, and then sent everyone home to discuss it with their families. He's thinking about it.

Lucy's mind goes into panic mode. He's only 51, and what's he going to do, sit at home?

He says they can do things that they always wanted. Lucy can't think of anything more claustrophobic. He never wanted to do anything when the kids were small, leaving her to do all the work, and now he expects her to drop everything?

The girls need to go to school, she says, and I have my work, too.

But you're only writing stuff. You can do that whenever you want.

No, she can't, because he will complain about it. He will complain about how much time she spends, and how much money, and will ask questions about the people she interacts with, and will continuously butt in and distract her, and then he will say that it's all "stuff for women" anyway as if that somehow makes it less important.

And it's not as if he will offer to get the girls from school, or do the cooking or the washing.

What on earth is she going to do?

She has an idea: she will tell him that since her business now supports the family, she wants to set it up as a business, with her own bank account and everything so that she can pay a monthly amount towards household expenses.

But is that the right thing to do? Of course she should have done this long ago, but she dislikes everything to do with money, and it was much easier to just let him handle it. But if he's going to sit at home, he's going to obsess over the money.

At the first opportunity, she goes to the author group, and asks: Does your partner support you?

The answers are quite interesting.

Tom says his wife has zero interest in his writing, but he started writing when he took time off from his work to look after her in her illness. She also understands that he needs something stimulating in his life. They are financially OK, but could use the money. Ultimately, his first priority will always be his wife and her deteriorating health.

Emily feels kind of trapped, because she started writing after an acrimonious divorce, and she hasn't been able to find a partner who understands her life. She really wants a bit more free time so she can rediscover other activities and find another partner in the first place, never mind whether he supports her.

Jack and Tony could use a bit more money. Tony works in a low-paying job and he would dearly like to go back to university but, at the moment, Jack's income isn't quite secure enough.

But it really depends on what sort of support you're talking about, Jack says.

And he continues:

As someone who has a fairly supportive family, and who did not have to make any major sacrifices in terms of work time, because I was self-employed anyway, I feel I'm not entirely qualified to talk about how to handle the lack of support by your family, and balancing their demands on your time.

But I have seen many of my friends struggle with this.

I also believe that support from a partner is a function of your overall love relationship dynamic, and your expectations of it.

My partner doesn't read anything of what I write. He is a reader of non-fiction, and does not read fiction at all. So it would be kind of torture for me to require him to read all my books. I'm not going to.

Yet I hear people finding it disturbing and disappointing that their partner doesn't read their books.

I don't believe that support by a partner means forcing them to read all the books I write. I believe that support by a partner is allowing the partner to do something they love, giving them the time and not subjecting them to emotional blackmail over time spent doing that thing.

Support is not standing by the sidelines and cheering. Frankly, that can be a little creepy. If that is your requirement in your life, that your partner cheers you all the way, then you really need to take a step back and consider what you would do if your partner forced you to do something they loved and you have no interest in.

At this point, Lucy remarks that she's not expecting that at all.

Tom says: I agree with Jack. Support is giving your partner the opportunities, not whining when they spend time doing the thing they love, not blackmailing them with conditions that have to be met before they can do this thing they love, not treating this thing that they love as something that is somehow going to stand in the way of the relationship, or holding financial conditions over their head.

At this point, Lucy starts feeling something bad in her bones. It has been there for a long time. Not only does her husband not really support her, but he's actively trying to blackmail her in subtle ways. If he's going to spend so much time at home, it's going to get infinitely worse to the point she's not sure she wants to be in that situation.

And it scares the pants off her.

Jack says to the group, not Lucy in particular:

Partner support and writing are going to be infinitely harder when you are struggling financially, or both of you have really busy jobs.

If you come up against a conflict, you may have to examine where your priorities lie for the time being. If you're both studying or working sixty-hour-per-week jobs so that you can get ahead and build a future together, demanding to take out a chunk of time to do something just for the love of it would sound selfish to the other partner. If you have really young children, there just may not be any time and emotional space to write. But children have a habit of growing up.

Many situations are temporary. It may not be the right time for you to be a writer.

If you want a writing career, you have to write. That's your job, and your partner should understand that.

Tom says that he agrees and that he expects writing to take a back seat for him for a little while.

Lucy says nothing. She is planning to go to the bank tomorrow morning.

TWENTY-THREE

Using a Developmental Editor

TOM FELT HE WASN'T getting anywhere. He had hoped that in addition to some extras in life, his writing would fund a trip to see his wife's brother, but he doesn't yet have enough money, his wife is not any getting better and her brother and his wife came to visit them instead.

Note for Tom: Priorities, mate!

It was a great week, in which his brother-in-law surprised him by saying how cool he thought it was that Tom was an author. He had read some of Tom's books—bought them, no less—and recommended them to his friends. Tom had noticed a flurry of sales in Greece on Google Play.

He was a bit embarrassed, because if Giorgios had told him, he'd have given him the books.

To make a long story short, now Tom has a little bit of money left over that he wants to use for his fiction.

He started publishing really set in his ways, but he's become convinced that some people he's been talking to may have a point. After all, he *did* model his books off some 1950s classics and he can see that modern fiction is different. Besides, he's had an idea to use his life experience of dealing with a sick relative in a new book. Not all space captains or hard-nosed detectives come without personal lives after all. He wants to make his fiction more real and less pew-pew.

He has also seen that his current books have some plotting and writing deficiencies. He never learned to write properly, and one doesn't rock up to a symphony orchestra expecting a job after two music lessons either. So at the very least he wants to do his best to fix his writing.

And prove that 62 is not old.

He scouts around for recommendations and hires Priya who lives in Sweden, but we won't hold that against her. She has a degree in Creative Writing, worked a bit for a big publisher until she married, moved to Sweden with her husband and had twins.

Note for writers like Tom: Check prospective editors' credentials. What qualifies them for the job?

Priya has a special interest in story structure and works mostly while the twins sleep. She also writes, but has put this on hold while the kids are little.

She uses Skype, which is something that Tom knows well, although he's never used it for anything to do with writing.

What does she tell Tom?

Potentially, there may be some hard truths for him to hear.

She says:

The writer's job

As a writer, when you're trying to persuade people to buy a book, you have a few things to play with. These are your cover, your blurb, and retailer specific things like categories and price point, and one of the most important ones, your sample.

Readers often look at the sample of the book that is available for free to check if they are likely to enjoy the rest of the book.

There are definite things that you can do that turn the reader away. This is not about the rules of writing, but it is about what makes people likely not to want to continue reading.

If your control of storytelling is poor, the reader will be confused. The reader might not know why they don't like the story, but it is not the reader's task to point this out to you. The reader only knows that they would prefer to read something else.

These are things in your style that may stop your readers:

Unengaging, stodgy prose

This is especially common to writers who have a fairly high level of education, and consider themselves professionals. (Tom falls squarely in that territory.)

In a lot of areas of work, like academia, wordiness is rewarded. Or, maybe I should rephrase that, wordiness is expected. If you are terribly wordy in your communication, you will look important. (Tom can totally relate to that.)

Whether people actually read your communication is another question. I wager that they probably don't. But much work, especially in larger organisations, relies on looking important. On selling yourself. It does not rely so much on whether people actually read your stuff.

When you start writing fiction, this will work against you. Readers are merciless, and will ditch any book that takes too much space to get to that point. Lean prose is always better than wordy prose.

Learn to cut out the flab. Look at your sentences to see which words are needed. You may need to ask an editor to guide you with this if you are doing this for the first time. And, yes, it may hurt, because the editor may tell you to get rid of word and phrase constructions that you have fallen in love with.

This brings us to another problem. There is a fair bit of repetition. If you fall in love with a type of sentence, your process becomes monotonous, sometimes even to a ridiculous level. Variety is king. You should never fall into the trap of doing the same thing over and over again.

Throat clearing clauses

"In the beginning, there was a book. Now you must know that this was a very bad book. When writing it, the officer had forgotten that he was not writing a technical manual."

Each of those three sentences includes a piece of throat clearing. We could clean this up by saying: "There was a book. It was a very bad book. The writer had forgotten he was not writing a technical manual."

The example above may seem a little sparse. If you cut out flabby words, you're likely to create a kind of staccato style that still has to be cleaned up. In the example above, I would probably choose to keep one of the short sentences. But I hope I've explained how a lot of extra words don't mean anything and just bog the reader down.

That was what it was verbiage

The phrase "that was what it was" is the ultimate string of empty words. Some writers of course will advise you to get rid of every instance of the word *that*. Try it, then give your piece to an editor, and you will find that the editor will put half of them back in. Words exist in the English language because they have a function. This means you will sometimes need them. But words like *that* and *was* and *what* easily become crutches for lazy writers who don't bother to find more specific terms. Be specific. Don't say "it" when you can mention what it is.

Poor point-of-view control

Modern books are almost all told in some form of "close" point-of-view. This can be third person or first person. It means the reader is in the head of a character throughout the story. A break of viewpoint happens when the reader is shown something that the character can't possibly see, or hear, or know. The reader gets confused and starts wondering whose story this is anyway. Do it too often, and you've lost them, and they can't even tell you why, just that they found reading too much hard work.

———

AFTER THE TALK, Tom contemplates that he's never had as much of a dressing-down from someone as nice, young and dark eyed and dark skinned as Priya. He thinks about the latter and concludes that it's important that Priya is totally not like him, because his readers are not like him, and in order to sell, he needs to think less like him and more like the readers.

He reads through the first chapter of his first book and finds so many of the things that she pointed out. He might as well toss the entire chapter and start over.

He really is a hack.

TWENTY-FOUR

Where To Begin

DURING THE NEXT meeting Priya goes on:

Beginning your book

Most beginning writers start their stories in the wrong place.

When I was reading for the publisher, I made a tally of all the submissions reviewed, and the reason I didn't think they were suitable for publication. You would expect a lot of the submissions to be badly written and full of mistakes, but that was only a very small percentage of them.

The biggest reason submissions were rejected was because the story was uninteresting. Specifically, the beginning was uninteresting.

The beginning of your book is extremely important. You have to start it in the right place, preferably where something happens that makes the reader take notice. It doesn't have to be "action" like a fight. Beginning writers also often make that mistake of inserting action before the reader knows—and recognises—the characters and cares about them. I'm not saying categorically that it *can't* be a fight or a long description of the scenery, but there has to be *something* in it that makes the reader want to read on. If anything, readers are less forgiving than they used to be, because there are thousands of other books they could read.

The other day I was listening to the Writing Excuses podcast. This is a show of short episodes that is very traditionally focused, but they also talk a lot about craft, especially story structure. This aspect is often overlooked by a lot of creative writing advice, which focuses on sentence structure.

One of the hosts asked: How do you make stories memorable? This is the Holy Grail. We want to write stories that people will remember, because if they do, they'll remember the author, they'll remember to check that author out, they'll recommend the author to their friends.

There is a sad tendency in the self-publishing writer space to be copycats. Well, I think it's sad anyway. The advice goes that you read bestselling books in your genre, write down the common plot elements, and use those in your book. If this is all you do, and it is indeed all a lot of people are doing, it will result in bland, cookie-cutter fiction that may sell reasonably well for a short period of time, but will otherwise be completely forgettable.

At the time Harry Potter came out there were already many books about young wizards who learned the craft of magic. In fact, it is entirely possible that some publishers were already saying "no more of this."

But the one thing Harry Potter did that none of the other books did was to add so much incredible detail to the world and how the characters interacted with that world. It made the concept *school for young magicians* its own.

The author took a concept that was beaten to death, and turned it into something so specific that it became alive to people.

"Muggles" has become an accepted word in everyday vocabulary.

The fact that she did this with a concept that was already tired shows that it doesn't really matter what setting you choose, but you have to own it and add something to it that's unique, and you have to do this from the beginning. Own it.

With that in mind, how should you structure the beginning of the story? One of the main problems with a lot of the submitted fiction I saw in my time as slush reader was that the story did not begin at the point where the plot began. We saw many stories with characters waking up and going about their daily business, and it took at least one scene to get into the reason for the story. The Look Inside on Amazon is a chapter at most. When you have only a few thousand words to play with, putting boring, everyday stuff there is a huge waste of space. The beginning of your book is the most important real estate that you have. Don't waste it with mundane things.

Deciding where to begin your story is the most important thing you can do.

TOM WRITES BACK: So you don't think I started the story in the right place?

Priya says: No, I don't think so. I think the story starts at the end of chapter three, because this is where the dramatic event occurs that changes the characters.

Tom is horrified. He says: but I need the stuff before that to explain how the world works.

And Priya says: You don't. Take it from me. I want you to take chapter three. Don't cut out the scene where he gets robbed. Rewrite it. Start the novel with the scene where the main character walks into the street and gets robbed. If the reader needs to know anything about the character, that he is half-robot and that the city is a metropolitan space station, this will come out in the scene or future scenes. Write the story so that you offer as little pre-explanation as possible, and offer it only when the reader absolutely needs to know it to understand the character's predicament.

Well, that's kind of annoying. Tom has spent the previous night cleaning up chapter one. And now it turns out he may not need it anymore, because he sees Priya's point. The story really does start at the end of chapter three.

TWENTY-FIVE

The Side Hustle

JACK IS FACING A PROBLEM.

This morning, their washing machine broke. It was already on its last legs and fixing it would be a waste of money for a small benefit. It's fifteen years old and would just break again.

They need to buy a new one.

But he also has a couple of expensive writing bills coming up. What can he do?

Piling some money on ads and selling more books is not the answer. That will just widen the financial hole. It's at least two months before the retailers pay, and the ad bill is due at the end of each month.

And to be honest, he's quite sick of the irregular and fickle nature of his writing income. One thing about Tony's shelf-stacking job is that the income is poor; the other is that it comes regularly.

Jack is seriously considering reviving his graphic design career.

He asks in the group: Do you have a side hustle?

According to the replies, quite a few people do.

This is the consensus:

A side hustle could solve some problems.

It may take a while to get your career off the ground. Maybe you are not a particularly fast writer. Maybe you hate marketing so much that it becomes an impediment to your sales. Maybe your career is taking too long to develop, and you need money more immediately. Maybe you want to use this money to buy better covers and better editing. Maybe you're plain bored of only writing.

Jack thinks: Yes to all those things.

He asks: What sort of things do people do?

The obvious ones are editing and cover design if you have any qualifications in those areas. Good cover designers are always in high demand. Cover design goes through phases and fashion, and if you can catch a wave and do it well, you can supplement your writing income in this way.

Things like speaking engagements and courses are more suitable to writers of non-fiction. But then again, maybe you have a specific field of knowledge from your previous job that you can use to write non-fiction. Non-fiction books are usually shorter and require less emotional energy to write.

Writers are hungry for knowledge, so if you can quickly write an informational guide on "The Writer's Guide To Airline Pilots", "Medical Terms For Writers", "What Writers Get Wrong About Farming" or something of that nature, go ahead and do it.

You could do website design for your fellow authors.

Quite a few people can do their own WordPress design, but there are others who lack the confidence or have additional money to pay someone to do it.

Commercial website design companies often charge too much, because their designs are tailored towards higher-end customers. Most writers just want a website that lists their books and has a form to sign up for their mailing list and maybe some information about themselves. These types of sites are hardly worth the effort of a full-fledged website design company.

If you write a lot and quickly, but you don't like plotting, you might find a second career as a ghostwriter. Many writers will pay well for those services.

If you have any training in audio production, you might find some money in becoming a narrator for food audiobooks. Especially if you are not in the top tier of charging narrators, there will be quite a steady market.

And you could become a personal or virtual assistant to other authors. Many of them will ask for someone to run their promotions, submit their books to promotion sites, run the Amazon and Facebook ads, run their mailing list and all kinds of things.

Since these are often well-selling authors, it is your opportunity to learn how to do these things. I don't need to tell you that this can be very beneficial.

All of these ideas for making extra income involve you trading off some of your time for a fixed income. This means that you will have less time for writing but, since it is nearly impossible to write all the time effectively for eight hours a day, it may be a worthwhile trade-off while you find your feet.

Having a side hustle is a little bit like having a day job. You need to carve out time for it, and this could force you to become more efficient in your writing. But since you will be working with other authors, it may also be beneficial for your writing career.

Jack is not the only one listening in on the discussion. He has already decided to put a selection of pre-made book covers on his website and is reasonably confident that he can find the audience who will buy enough to give him a little extra cash this month.

But Emily is also watching. She likes the option of becoming a ghostwriter. How easy would it be to receive a plot, write the book in a week or two and be handed a few thousand dollars guaranteed? No marketing skill required.

Even Tom is thinking that he might be able to turn his knowledge about science into a book that helps writers get things right.

TWENTY-SIX

What If I'm Not Good Enough?

LUCY IS PREPARING for the launch of her new series. It's another historical romance, but she has started to have serious doubts about whether it will do well. That troll who left one-star reviews on her books is still out there. Amazon hasn't taken down the reviews. What if she returns and dumps a one-star review on the new book? Lucy has been a bit late completing the book and there isn't the time to send the book off to readers before it goes live. All this stress with the group and then the situation with her husband just makes her want to crawl into a hole.

She asks a question in the group: Do you ever feel you're not good enough?

The replies blow her away.

Even the most accomplished, best-selling writers in the group admit that they often feel this way. That someone will come along, pierce their bubble and say: Look, you were a fraud after all. Now go back to your office cubicle.

It's astonishing.

Not even getting a traditional publishing deal does anything to alleviate it. Jack says he started his publishing career by landing a deal with a traditional publisher. Reflecting on why he signed the deal—knowing it wasn't going to make him a lot of money—was that he needed validation.

But validation is a trap, says another group member known for hard-hitting replies. The need for validation can also be labelled "self-doubt".

If being rejected by agents and publishers makes you feel like a bad writer, then I have some news for you: the fact that some of your books are ranked in the millions on Amazon will also make you feel like a bad writer. Not only that, but you will continue to feel this way, because there will always be people who do better than you, there will always be bad reviews, and rankings go up and down naturally.

If your happiness depends on external factors, whether they be a publisher's nod, an agent's accolades, a good review in *Publishers Weekly*, 500 five-star reviews on Amazon, or whatever else you can dream up then you will be set up for a lot of disappointment.

This is the truth: external validation is a fallacy.

It may exist for short periods of time, but supposing you landed a really good deal, and the publisher paid you six figures for the book you haven't yet written and hasn't hit the shelves, you will just replace it by the next validation parameter that your overactive mind dreams up.

What if I can't make my deadline? What if I can't get the book to be as I want? What if I don't like the editor of the publishing house? What if they give you a horrible cover? What if the book doesn't sell? What if the industry magazines give it horrible reviews?

It is not hard to see that this process goes on and on.

Then you self-publish and similar types of doubts bubble to the surface: what if no one buys the book; what if my reviews are bad; what if my readers hate it?

If you're going to wait for these kinds of external parameters to prove whether or not you're good enough, you are going to wait forever. Validation is rubbish, and you should forget about it right now.

Well, Lucy scoffs. She finds the response a bit rude, to be honest. It's not like she can turn off a feeling that she has.

No you can't, the writer agrees.

But you should manage it so it doesn't destroy you. You should undertake all the steps that you feel are necessary to put out a book of decent quality. Then you should quit looking for validation.

It means taking some hard steps. It may mean dropping out of that community of writers who judge others by the size of their publishing deals. It may mean not looking at your reviews for a while, or ignoring your sales dashboard at times when you know sales are going to be slow. It may mean not interacting with certain people who make you feel bad about yourself.

This will be hard when those people are close to you, but in some way you have to carve out some space for yourself. If you can't find the space, you may need to assess who you associate with.

It is really hard to talk about these kinds of things. It's common, for almost every writer, to be worried about how the new long-planned release will do. If it does poorly then you have just wasted a couple of months of your life writing this book. That really sucks.

But ultimately, you can't control the reaction to your books. If you're looking at your reviews for validation, you will not find it, because there will always be bad reviews.

Some writers with self-doubt find it therapeutic to go to the page of a very successful book in your genre. Have a look at the 1-star reviews. Read what people have said about those books that have sold millions of copies. Not everyone will like everything. You can do nothing about it.

Lucy knows full well that the need to be liked, to get good reviews, to quell disunity in her groups, is destroying her, because she can't do and be everything. People jokingly call her a mother hen, and that's what she is: making sure that none of her babies—her real life ones or her book babies—suffer any bad experiences.

And now her husband is throwing a spanner into the works by giving her less time and looking over her shoulder. He wants to be another baby she needs to mind.

It's late at night when she's reading this, and she's crying at the computer. Maybe she should give the whole thing up and go be a dutiful housewife.

What is most distressful to her is that she knows what she has to do, and that she has a tendency to take far too many things too personally, but still the despair surfaces at the most inopportune moments, such as just before a new release.

TWENTY-SEVEN

Refresh Your Work

TOM HAS SPENT a few weeks rewriting his three books.

Self-publishing gives you the freedom to change anything about your book at any time. A lot of writers try different covers, and some even edit and re-edit their books several times.

Is this worth doing?

He's about to find out.

Lucy feels quite uncertain about those first books that she wrote. She has learned much as a writer and every time she looks at those first books she cringes and wishes to unpublish them. To make matters worse, they're still selling. Or does that really make matters worse?

To Lucy, it's an embarrassment. To the readers, it's obviously not.

A number of Lucy's friends have rebranded their books. Is it a good idea for her to do this?

In the author group, Luke says:

Rebranding a book can be a good idea for a number of reasons.

First, to make sure that all books in the series look similar and that you can easily tell that it is a series. This is very important and always worth doing.

Second, when you have a feeling that the covers currently on your books mislead people about the genre or the type of content. This may be worth doing, but it carries the risk that you're wrong. It wouldn't be the first time that I have seen this happen to people.

People also rebrand their books because they feel that the old versions of the book were not up to scratch. Since this is so highly subjective, I don't think it is worth doing, especially in Lucy's case, where the books are still selling. I've seen many writers ruin reasonably respectable sales figures by pulling the books, rewriting and republishing them.

Since it is hard to determine what attracts readers to a particular book, it may be that your rejigging of the content upset something and you may lose your sales. If you have any kind of sales, don't touch existing work. Yes, it's likely that if you are doing all the right things and you're learning about your fiction, you will learn a lot and your earlier books will make you cringe. But this doesn't mean that by supposedly fixing them with things you have learned you will necessarily improve their sales. I have almost never seen this happen. If you have done the right thing and have learned to write better books, then use that knowledge to write more and better books, but don't touch your existing books.

If you're really so embarrassed by a book you have published that you don't want to see it any more, simply unpublish it. But I would advocate very much against doing so unless the book also doesn't sell at all. As long as the book is selling it means that people enjoy it and they don't see all the things that you see wrong with it. You don't know what attracts readers to a book, so don't try to second-guess because you will get it wrong. Practice your new skills on a new book.

To sum up:

- Recover and refresh the presentation of your books if it brings them into line with their series or genre.
- Don't rewrite existing books. If they sell, it's likely to kill sales. If they don't sell, you just waste time.

But Tom goes ahead and tries anyway.

TWENTY-EIGHT

The Ups and Downs

IT'S D-DAY.

Tom's newly rewritten series goes live.

Lucy also has a new release.

Jack has set up a page and his cover design business goes live.

Emily launches new books all the time, but today, her KDP Select term expires and she's going to start selling books wide.

Tom is using his mailing list to announce the revamped series. He knows that the people on the list are likely to already have read the book, so a friend in the author group has agreed to send a notification to his list as well. He's made the first book 99¢ and booked a few promotion sites.

Apart from using her list, Lucy is planning to put some notifications on her Facebook reader group, and she knows she will get a lot of sales from it, but oh dear, why is it that when she planned this release date, she didn't check the school calendar. It's school holidays! Her girls are at home.

It's around mid-morning and she has just made some coffee

when she hears a crash outside, followed by crying. A moment later, her oldest comes running into the house. Her sister has fallen off her bike and hurt herself. Lucy rushes outside to find her girl—and bike—at the bottom of the patio steps, clutching her arm. One look, and it's clear: it's obviously broken.

Lucy jumps in the car and takes both girls to the hospital, where a long cycle of waiting ensues. She worries about her release. She rings her husband, but when she asks if he can come home earlier from work—that he still hasn't notified about his interest in taking the exit package—he's evasive and talks about meetings. What about her release and the emails she needs to send?

So much for wanting to spend more time at home.

In the group, Luke says:

Writing is a very fickle business. You can be selling gangbusters one day and then all of a sudden for some reason not clear, the wheels fall off, sales drop and you have to do something to rescue your career. It could be something simple, or it could be something you don't even know how to begin to diagnose.

Many writers can be hit hard when Amazon changes certain things, I have seen them get burnt out, I have seen people have great hopes for a new series which flopped, and I have seen people simply wanting to do something else.

The fact is that if you sell at a certain level, there is absolutely no guarantee that this will continue. Writing is a creative career, and it is fraught with ups and downs. The sooner you realise this, the better.

There is only one foolproof prediction of sales, and this is zero: your book will always get at least . . . zero sales. If you've been around for a bit and people know you, there will be at least some sales, but beyond that, no one can predict sales, especially not for a new project.

This is quite discomfiting to a lot of people. New writers may even get angry. What do you mean all of a sudden my audience will just pack up and leave and my sales will be back down to the same levels as when I began?

It happens. The best way to deal with it is to be prepared. Or, should I say, don't ever expect it never to happen.

Emily can feel that uncertainty right now. In between uploading her books to other retailers, she's checking her sales, and there aren't many to speak of. She's been told that sales on other retailers will take a bit longer to show up.

She did get an email from her fan Chris, who said that she's very happy that she can finally buy Emily's books on Apple, and that she has done so. The sale takes more than a day to show up, and then there is only one. Emily is not calling this a great success. Yes, she needs to have patience. She's budgeted six months for this. No need to get anxious yet, right? Right?

Jack is doing better. His site launch has resulted in four cover orders, and it looks like he won't have to forego anything in order to buy a new washing machine.

Considering the circumstances, Tom is reasonably happy with his relaunch. No, it didn't smash any records, but he's sold more than he has for a long time, even if most of the sales were at 99¢. He's also still a long way in the hole after paying Priya, but he feels he's getting somewhere. He accepts Luke's point that the best place to show off his new skills is in the next book. He quietly unpublishes the fourth book, because he can see that if that series is ever going to be successful, he needs to gut it, but he wants to think about starting something else. He doesn't know what it's going to be yet. At the moment, his mind is occupied. After a brief period at home, Helena is back in the hospital, and he fears she may not come out again.

And Lucy?

Her daughter is fine.

But when she comes home at six, her launch emails still unsent and her phone buzzing with "where are you?" messages from her readers, she finds that her husband has been home but has gone again. To the gym probably. The milk is sitting out on the table, everything she needs to cook is still solid frozen and the back door is wide open.

She's fuming.

TWENTY-NINE

Change Direction

ENOUGH FAFFING.

Emily has finished uploading all her books to all retailers. She's watching her sales like a hawk, and it's discouraging, because after a little flurry of sales, things have dried up again, and to make matters worse, she's received an email from a reader asking why she can no longer read the books in Kindle Unlimited. Emily resists snapping back with: Because I got bills to pay.

But it wouldn't be the truth. She's got money saved. It's just that all this doing nothing stresses her out. She's going to start on a new project. Also, she clearly needs a plan to increase her sales on other retailers.

Even if Jack's brief foray into cover design had the desired result, the effect is short-lived, and he still has to face the fact that his catalogue is scattered and that his ad costs keep increasing. The effect is masked briefly because he has one ad that's particularly successful, but it addresses none of the underlying issues: he needs to get his act together and write the books that need to be written. But the ultimate issue is that he's not a fast writer. He needs to do research and he needs a few weeks' worth of zero-stress time so that he can get a first draft done.

While Tom drives to and from the hospital and sits in waiting rooms, he thinks about future projects. How about he writes a book about a space captain with an elderly mother on board? Or someone with a serious health issue? In a spacefaring future, not everyone is going to be healthy. But he can already hear Priya's voice: that sounds like a for-the-love project. You shouldn't stop writing them, but they probably won't help your bank balance.

Then what?

Lucy is trying to salvage her disastrous launch.

She explains the situation to her readers, and they're all very sympathetic. The book is a bit slow off the mark, but sales pick up soon enough.

Her writing is fine. Her marketing is fine. The underlying issue that she needs to address is: she has to stop freaking out about everything.

And somehow she needs to make her husband understand that there are four people in the family. If he wants to work less, he's going to have to pick up some slack at home. After all, she's done that for years.

She needs a plan.

She asks in the group: how many writers here are full-time and how are you doing?

There are some heartwarming and spectacular stories going around of writers who walked into their boss' office and told them where to stick their crappy jobs and never looked back. Those are awesome stories.

However, the reality is, that "going full-time" looks much more mundane for most writers:

- They gradually transition into full-time writing, for example teachers scaling back hours
- They are retired and don't need to work
- They lost their jobs
- They haven't worked for a long time because they've been caring for relatives, or because they live in a job-poor area, or because they've got health issues which make them near-unemployable
- They're supported by partners
- They have alternate income

A writer named Debra says: Going fulltime is a chicken-and-egg situation. And I have to—unabashedly gleefully—admit that it's just about the only career where the traditionally disadvantaged are at an advantage: if you're old, unemployed or unemployable, this world really is your oyster. (Debra uses a wheelchair)

Luke adds:

If you're the main breadwinner for a family of four, two dogs and a healthy mortgage, then, yep, you're going to have to pee your pants about going full-time. You want a big buffer. You want a family member picking up the slack, if at all possible. You can make a trade off: how about you spend a few years furthering your career full-time in the workforce while I drop off and pick up the kids, drive them to soccer, do the washing, go to the post office and do the shopping. Oh, wait. I'm meant to write.

You could downsize. Get rid of the mortgage. Move to a cheaper area. Move to a cheaper country. For Americans: move to a country where healthcare is universal and cheap or free.

Another writer says: For many beginning writers going full-time as an author is the big dream. For quite a few, having reached that lofty goal, they find that they don't like it and go back to some form of paid employment.

There are a few things about writing full-time that you must know.

It is a terribly lonely existence. You spend a lot of time by yourself with your computer, looking at your screen. You can go to a cafe or some other place where you are surrounded by people, but this won't mitigate that you are not talking to people, or that your productive time is spent alone. You may not be the right type of person to do this.

Some people do collaborations with other writers. This may work.

As soon as you spend a significant amount of time at home, all the other people who live in your house will start dumping domestic tasks on you. Because you are at home, you wouldn't mind going to the post office, doing the shopping, staying at home so that a parcel can be delivered, talking to the lawn-mowing guy, and making sure that the pool is free of leaves.

Because you're at home anyway and have nothing to do, right?

Yes, that's the issue Lucy needs to address, besides a few others. She has done a poor job of managing her finances, because she's had her husband to rely on. She's recently opened her own bank account, but there is more to be done. Because even if Lucy has written full-time for a while, she plans to go full-time financially. What shape that will take will depend on her husband.

THIRTY

Make a Plan

THE DREADED P-WORD. Jack hates it.

He's never had a plan and he sucks at plans and, even right now, he's being pulled in two directions. It would make excellent sense to finish those series, and he will do that. Eventually.

But he's recently received an email from a company that wants to put his best-selling book out in audio. He's been hearing a lot of good things about audio books. In his many half-arsed careers, he used to work for a radio station, and he reckons he can record audio books. His own audio books, because he's not going to go into any deals with other people. The last time he handed his books to someone else, it didn't end so well, so he prefers to record his own.

Well, that's a plan, of sorts. Record his books in audio. Finish the damn series.

Tom's plan is to do something with what he has learned about writing engaging fiction.

Because his mental space was so crowded with hospitals and

doctors, he has no ideas of anything else to write, so he plots a story about the space captain with the elderly ill mother. But a little voice in his head that sounds like Priya tells him that this kind of thing is not going to appeal to a lot of people.

But something else happens.

He is waiting somewhere, leafing through books to buy on his tablet when a book comes up in the science fiction list that is so ridiculous, the description made him laugh out loud. He bought the book—by an author he'd never heard of—and laughed his way through it. Not only that, when he finished, his first thought was: I could totally write something like this. He knows about science and chemical reactions. It will be a story about space scientific officer goofballs who stuff up everything in science labs. Of course, when you're in space, unexpected chemical reactions have even more impact. Out in space, no one can smell your rotten eggs.

Tom doesn't quite know what's going to be the main plot of the story yet—a major departure from his usual way of thinking—but he knows a number of the funny scenes that happen.

Emily's plan involves figuring out how to get people on other retailers to start buying her books. She's already lost a month worth of sales and she's getting antsy. Her mailing list is growing, and they appear to like it that the books are everywhere, so maybe she should work harder on that. She also figures that if she continues to write a book every 6–8 weeks, there will be no need to send chatty emails. She can just announce the books to her list.

She has also decided to launch new books in KU for three or six months, since she knows how to give them a good headstart, and she sees many other writers doing this.

But meanwhile, she has been replying to at least one fan each day, and she's added a few features to her website.

Her cat has obtained a section in her newsletters. With every announcement, she posts a picture of something silly she has caught him doing (yes, cats really do drink out of the toilet). People seem to like it.

Her plan also involved taking at least one night per week off and doing something non-writing related with her time. She always enjoyed plays, so she's joined the drama society. It's actually fun looking at a story in another way. She might learn something new she can use in her fiction. And, you know, talking to normal people.

Lucy is almost done setting up her business. She's managed to salvage most of her ruined release, and found that, although it can be fun, a Facebook release party doesn't really add that much in terms of sales. Her husband hasn't mentioned taking up an exit offer again. She hopes he realises she's busy.

There is a lot of discussion about publishing plans in the author group. Some new writers are planning twelve-book series, and Tom feels proud to say that he was once planning a very long series, but now he understands why designing a series like this might not be a good idea (if it sells and it grows that way, that's another matter).

Luke says:

It is important to have a plan. The plan may be that you write a series in one genre, then write another series in a slightly different sub genre and make the first books free to advertise them. The plan may be that you write a book a month in a particular genre and the only advertising you will do is writing another book.

You may need to think about what you will do when your chosen strategy doesn't work out as well as you hoped.

You may need to think about a number of alternative directions you could take. Another genre, preferably one that is fairly closely related, or one that is really close to your heart.

You could try another pen name, hopefully attracting a different audience.

You could try advertising and cross-promotion. You should always have a mailing list, but you can put more emphasis on it, or you can go in a different direction altogether.

If you still have a day job, this will be easier for you, because you will have less time to play with, so you have to make hard choices. Since, if you have less time, those choices will be towards writing more books, it is natural that for the amount of time spent writing, you will have more books than someone who does it full time and has to contend with all the marketing.

Then Lucy asks Luke: what is your plan? Because Luke earns more money writing than all of them could ever attain combined.

He says: I plan to retire early, buy a boat and marry the mother of my stepson.

An admirable goal, they all agree. There is no point to being a writer if you can't also be happy.

THE NEXT SUBJECT: How much time should your plan include for doing marketing?

The group concludes: this will depend on a number of things. Your writing speed for one, but also how well your books normally sell.

If you sell well, the temptation is not to do any marketing. But the danger is that at some point your sales are going to plummet. It always happens unexpectedly, and usually it's not a gradual process. Once the retailer sites stop showing your book to prospective buyers, sales drop off very quickly. If you have never spent any time thinking about or practising the various ways you can market your books, you are going to be at a significant disadvantage to people who might have sold much less than you, but who have had to market for every single book sale.

The advantage you will have, if you use it well, is that you already have a style or subject matter that people like. But by changing tack and writing yet another series, there is also a chance that you throw this advantage out the window.

No matter how much success you have currently, you should always keep your eye on the future. What if your sales start declining?

If your books never sold that well, at least you don't have this problem. You have always had to market for every single sale.

It's funny that writers like to be given a percentage that they "should" spend marketing. They want to hear that it is 10% or 20% or 50% or whatever. The truth is that this will vary per person, it will vary depending on your current situation. It goes without saying that around a new release you will spend a lot more time marketing then you will when you're writing something new.

But ultimately, marketing should never come at excessive cost to your production schedule.

If you're spending so much time marketing that you don't have time to write, something is wrong.

In that case, you may need to look at your audience, your fiction, and your targeting.

Marketing should not need to take over your entire life.

A book that hits the audience well and is well received shouldn't need a huge amount of marketing. If you feel your current series is constantly pushing sludge uphill, you're probably better off trying again with a different series.

Park your current series wide, make the first book free, use it to attract subscribers to your mailing list, but then stop all the other marketing and write something new. For most writers this is going to be the default course of action.

If however you find that the little marketing you do is very successful, do more of it.

If it feels like hard work for little reward, do less of it.

Those principles should be engraved on the writers' foreheads.

THERE IS NO NORM.

Groups of well-connected writers often gravitate towards their "norm" of best practices. People in the group will tell newcomers that they "must" do this or that.

Luke cautions against this way of thinking.

He says: When I first started publishing, things were different; so I can tell someone what I did, but they wouldn't be successful by doing what I did, and it wouldn't be relevant. Sadly, a lot of people look up to certain people so much that they seem unable to think for themselves. Everyone in this group should know that circumstances change all the time and are absolutely not the same as last year. I know squat about making it as a new writer today.

Jack jokes: So we should all leave?

Luke says: You shouldn't take what I say as gospel. Or anything anyone else says. Think for yourself. Your path will not be the same as your neighbour's.

THIRTY-ONE

Where are they now?

WHERE DOES this leave our writers? Where are they now?

AFTER SIX YEARS of illness and a month in a hospice, Helena passed away peacefully. Tom was devastated, but found solace in a small community of writers. This is also where he met Dave and Susan, a couple in exactly the same situation. He's helping them through hardship for when Susan will succumb to her illness.

It changed his outlook on life.

His work with Priya paid off. He wrote, in short succession, a series about romping space scientists that just took off—well, at least compared to his other books. He put it in Kindle Unlimited, made some good money, but he's now ready to take it out.

The money helped him sell his house and move closer to his daughter.

He then wrote his idea of a space captain who deals with his dying mother aboard his ship, and he cried every page of the book. In the end, the sales weren't terribly great, but the book earned out and he wanted to write it. He's convinced he can write another book and is planning to use some of his money to go travelling.

WHEN EMILY TOOK her books out of Kindle Unlimited, it was terrible. But she persevered, and now she has a growing income that doesn't depend on her churning out a book every month. It's a long-term project, but it's going in the right direction. She has more time to do other things. The reader Chris has become a friend.

She met a nice guy at the drama society. Trouble is, he comes with two little girls and a dog that really doesn't like her cat. Fun times ahead!

JACK HAS BEEN busy finishing some of his projects. It's a hard slog, but he's getting there.

But he's finding it hard to let go of his advertising addiction. He's set a time limit to how much time he's allowed to work on it over working on new books.

His completed series relaunch gives him reason for hope. That did better than he expected.

He recorded his books in audio, and they now give him some welcome extra income.

Unfortunately, Tony got laid off from work and they went through a hard couple of months. Jack tried to get Tony to do his ads, but that didn't work out, so he decided instead to cut down on his writing and take up more cover design work. He's done that before, and the income is a lot steadier. They moved to a cheaper apartment and he sent Tony to get the degree he always wanted.

On a romantic visit to the beach, he proposed to Tony, and they now have a wedding to plan.

They're moving ahead, even if there will be no money to get a dog for a while.

———

THE DAY LUCY found out her husband was having an affair, she bundled the kids into the car and left for her mother. The next day, she went to the bank and changed the address on her accounts and took his name off them.

He begged her to come back, but for her, this was it.

She was so upset that she didn't write anything for six months. Her sales suffered, but fortunately, she still had her supportive communities.

She's started writing again. She cares less about what people think, because she no longer has someone who measures her worth by her sales. She'll be starting a new series, and she has great hopes for it.

———

WHAT ABOUT YOU, author-reader?

If you've read all the way, you will know that there are no endlessly upward trajectories or perpetually happy endings. There are only happy people. Nothing is ever permanent. Both good and bad things happen all the time. The saying goes: if you're handed lemons, you make lemonade. It's about the journey, not the destination. I could go on and on, piling on clichés and mangling bad metaphors. However, the clichés wouldn't have become clichés if they weren't true.

THESE ARE the things that are true:

Be happy

You have to enjoy what you're doing now. Not some time in the future. You have to enjoy the process, the learning, trying new things. There is no easy button. There is no reward for hard work if you hate the work. That's just not worth it.

Keep learning

Always do this. It doesn't matter what shape it takes, but don't get stale. Don't keep doing the same thing over and over and expect different results. Keep an open mind.

Try stuff . . .

Always try new things. A new writing process, new advertising, a new genre or pen name, heck, even going back to basics. Try it.

. . . even if people say it won't work

If you really like to do it, try it anyway. Don't listen to the naysayers. If you have a plan, it may just work. Or it may not, and you may learn something else that turns out to be valuable. The naysayers are not you. They know nothing about you and your circumstances.

Remember the economics

This is vitally important: always spend less than you earn. If you suddenly have a few good months, invest the money. Don't just go and spend it all. Save up for the future.

Do more of what works

This should be obvious, but it's amazing how many writers spend huge amounts of effort and time chasing sales for books that have a hard time getting off the ground, or series with poor sell-through rates. If you want to invest, pick the part of your business that works best and invest in that.

Do less of what doesn't

This should also be obvious, but writers need a reminder that it's OK not to do stuff that doesn't work for them at that point in time. "Stuff that doesn't work" includes stuff you hate.

Consider the needs of others

Like those in your family. There may be times that they are more important than writing. That's OK. There may be times that you need money and it's easier to do some work-for-hire project that delivers a fixed income. Nothing wrong with that either.

Don't forget to enjoy yourself

Ultimately, you got into writing because you wanted to. If it starts feeling too much like the cubicle desk job that you hated, something is off. You are your own boss. You get to make the rules.

———

THAT'S PRETTY MUCH IT. Now go forth and write.

About the Author

Patty Jansen lives in Sydney, Australia, where she spends most of her time writing Science Fiction and Fantasy.

Her story *This Peaceful State of War* placed first in the second quarter of the Writers of the Future contest and was published in their 27th anthology. She has also sold fiction to genre magazines such as Analog Science Fiction and Fact, Redstone SF and Aurealis.

Patty has written over twenty novels in both Science Fiction and Fantasy, including the *Icefire Trilogy* and the *Ambassador* series.

pattyjansen.com

Books by Patty Jansen

MORE INFORMATION:
PATTYJANSEN.COM

www.ingramcontent.com/pod-product-compliance
Lightning Source LLC
Chambersburg PA
CBHW071500080526
44587CB00014B/2167